Answers to Alleged
101 Contradictions in the Bible

ANSWERS TO ALLEGED 101 CONTRADICTIONS IN THE BIBLE

ORIEL BELTRAN
DUMANON

XULON PRESS

Xulon Press
2301 Lucien Way #415
Maitland, FL 32751
407.339.4217
www.xulonpress.com

Printed in the United States of America.

ISBN-13: 978-1-54563-632-9

Acknowledgments

I would like to give my acknowledgments and thanks to the following people:

The first person I would like to give acknowledgment to is Mr. Rick Meyers, the creator of e-sword. This FREE Bible software has so much treasure of Bible versions, commentaries, dictionaries and other Bible helps, it is unbelievable that he has made this app FREE until now. e-Sword has made it so much easier for me to search for answers to questions of the alleged contradictions in the Bible. In e-Sword, whatever Bible verse you click on, automatically displays the discussion, observation and explanation from various Bible commentaries. Without Rick's unique work, it would have been very tedious and time consuming for me to finish this dissertation. I highly recommend it to every serious student of the Bible. And, did I mention it is FREE? Download this amazing app with all its FREE add-ons, right from http://www.e-sword.net. My using e-Sword Bible software explains why abbreviations of Bible books in quoting scriptures in this research may differ from other works.

To Norman L. Geisler and Thomas Howe, authors of *The Big Book of Bible Difficulties*. This is my "go to" book. If there is an alleged contradiction that I cannot find discussed in this book, I go to look in the Bible commentaries and dictionaries in e-Sword and other resources.

To my darling daughter, Charlyn Lez D. Moss and to a dear brother in Christ, Pastor Abelito Suizo, for reading the original manuscript, editing it and making suggestions to improve it.

To Dr. Jeff Victor, president of Summit Bible College (Bakersfield, CA) for the encouragement he gave me to undertake this work as a doctoral dissertation.

To my beloved DCI Family (Destiny Center International), the church I pastor in Bakersfield, CA for graciously allowing me to use part of my time to work on this book.

Most of all, to our Great God and Savior, Jesus Christ, Who sent His Holy Spirit to help me in writing this book.

Introduction

Why *Answers to Alleged 101 Contradictions in the Bible*

One day, a member of our church gave me an article entitled, "*101 Contradictions in the Bible*." It was given to him by a co-worker in the company he's working in. I had no ready answers to those questions except for those which are theological in nature.

I believe the Bible is the revealed will of God to His creation, so it must be true. There must be answers to these questions, though I did not yet know them then. Because I was certain those questions could be answered soundly, that article did not change my conviction about the veracity of the Bible.

Later on, I learned that some believers, including some ministers of the gospel, actually wanted to know the answers to these questions themselves. What made matters worse was that, I heard that the mother of the church member who gave me a copy of the article, was concerned that her son might embrace another faith. Her fears might have been unfounded, but her concern added to the reasons for me to search in earnest for the answers to these nagging questions.

Motives for Writing

I noticed that the copy of "*101 Contradictions in the Bible*" given me had no author. I thought this is good. In the culture I grew up with, many times proving a statement as wrong was understood as going against the person making the statement. I have no motive of going against the writer of "*101 Contradictions in the Bible*." My Bible tells me to love everyone. My simple motive was to find the answers to these questions, because personally, for me, the answers would add to my knowledge and understanding on the contents of the Bible. This knowledge would, in turn, help me explain to or teach others on the truth in the Bible. [Note: When I was almost finished answering the *"101 Contradictions in the Bible,"* I saw this same article in pdf form on the internet for all the public to read or download free. Here are three links with no by-lines for the author: http://media.isnet.org/kmi/off/XXtian/101ContradictionsInTheBible.pdf and http://ebooks.rahnuma.org/religion/Christianity/101%20Contradictions%20In%20The%20Bible.pdf, and http://internationalindigenoussociety.com/wp-content/plugins/pdfjs-viewer-shortcode/pdfjs/web/viewer.php?file=http%3A%2F%2Finternationalindigenoussociety.com%2Fwp-content%2Fuploads%2F2017%2F04%2F101-Contradictions-In-The-Bible.pdf&download=true&print=true&openfile=false. These two links do have by-lines: http://sunnahonline.com/ilm/dawah/0009.htm and http://www.answering-christianity.com/101_bible_contradictions.htm.]

What This Work Means To Me

I thank God for the person who prepared the *"101 Contradictions in the Bible."* I did not even notice most of these seeming problems in the Bible except for a common few and especially those which are theological in nature. After being able to answer all of them, I felt good inside knowing I now have something to share to those who want answers to these questions. This has also strengthened further my conviction on the truthfulness and divine origin of the Bible. I trust this work would mean as much to those who will read it as it does to me.

Alleged Contradiction # 1

1. Who incited David to count the fighting men of Israel?
   (a) God did (2 Sam. 24:1)
   (b) Satan did (1 Chron. 21:2)

Answer:

In 1 Corinthians 10:13, we read: No temptation has overtaken you except such as is common to man; but <u>God</u> *is* faithful, who <u>will not allow you to be tempted beyond what you are able</u>, but with the temptation will also make the way of escape, that you may be able to bear *it.* NKJV

The Bible teaches that God will not allow man to be tempted beyond what he is able to bear and when God does allow it, He also provides a way of escape. This means Satan, the tempter, can only do to man what God permits him to do. This is illustrated in the story of Job. In Job Chapter 1, Satan accused God that Job was serving Him only because of His protection upon his life and the prosperity He has blessed him with. So, God permitted Satan to take away Job's donkeys, sheep, camels, servants and even his children but did not allow Satan to touch Job himself (v. 12). In spite of these, Job continued to worship God (vv. 21, 22). In Chapter 2, when Satan was again in the presence of God, God said to him that "you incited **me** against him (Job) to destroy him without a cause" (v. 3). Here God, as the One who permitted Satan to destroy Job, said of Himself as the One who destroyed Job without a cause, though it was Satan who actually did it to Job. So, in answer to the supposed contradiction # 1, it was Satan who actually incited King David (according to 1 Chron. 21:2) and God is said to have done it (2 Chron. 24:1) because He gave permission to Satan to do it. The reason God gave permission to Satan to incite David and, in a sense gave His approval, is explained by a Bible commentary this way: "There were festering in David's heart a thirst for war, and pride in his victories; a growing ambition, and, as its necessary result, a disregard of the rights of other nations. The same passions were gaining a daily increasing influence over the people generally. It is too often the case that a nation uses the bravery which has obtained for it freedom from foreign oppression, to impose the yoke of slavery upon others."[1] This implies that God, Who knows our hearts, can allow specific temptations to come, so we can learn and be strengthened against them, as necessary for our spiritual growth.

---

[1] H D M. Spence and J. Exell, *The Pulpit Commentary.* (Grand Rapids: Eerdmans Publishing Company, 1950). Notes on 2 Samuel 24:1

2. In that count how many fighting men were found in Israel?
   (a) Eight hundred thousand (2 Samuel 24:9)
   (b) One million, one hundred thousand (1 Chron. 21:5)

3. How many fighting men were found in Judah?
   (a) Five hundred thousand (2 Sam. 24:9)
   (b) Four hundred and seventy thousand (1 Chron. 21:5)

Answer:

The above two supposed contradictions use the same Bible references so we'll answer them together. It would be best to answer the # 3 Alleged Contradiction first: How many fighting men were found in Judah? The answer in 1 Chron. 21:5 is 470,000 or 30,000 less than what is found in 2 Sam. 24:9. Let us first understand that when King David began his reign, the ten tribes of Israel in the north did not immediately submit to him, but they had Ishbosheth, a son of King Saul as their king and called their kingdom as Israel. The two tribes in the southern part were Judah and Benjamin and called themselves as Judah. 1 Chron. 21:5 says that "all Israel" (northern and southern part) had 1,100,000 soldiers and says "and Judah had 470,000" without using the word "all" in Judah. In a pre-vious event, when David wanted to bring the Ark of God from Baalah in Judah (in the frontiers of Philistine country where the Ark was at that time) to Jerusalem, he gathered 30,000 able men from Israel (See 2 Sam. 6:1). This troop were not only from Judah alone but from the whole nation of Israel which includes the northern part. Since these fighting men had already been counted and since they are not composed of people from Judah alone, the writer of 1 Chron. 21:5 did not include them in the new counting of fighting men ordered by King David; thus number for Judah is 470,000 or 30,000 less than In 2 Sam. 24:9. 2 Sam. 24:9 has 500,000 because the writer here as we can clearly read in this verse refers to all in the southern part of the kingdom of David in comparison to all in the northern part.[2]

Now let us answer the supposed contradiction # 2: How many fighting men were found in Israel? 2 Sam. 24:9 says 800,000 and 1 Chron. 21:5 says 1,100,000. Let us remember again that in 1 Chron. 21:5 (a later writing), the verse says "in all Israel" (not just the northern part of the nation which was also called Israel) and, therefore, already "including 470,000 in Judah" while in 2 Sam. 24:9 it only says, "in Israel" and "in Judah" making it clear as referring to the northern part and the southern part of the nation. Actually, there were two reports by Joab to the King. The first was an itemized report (in 2 Sam. 24:9) which had 800,000 for Israel and 500,000 for Judah (totaling 1,300,000 in all). In the second report (as written in 1 Chron. 21:5), it was the sum total of all In the nation of Israel. This second report was only 1,100,000 in all of Israel instead of 1.300,000. But this seeming discrepancy is quickly explained by the writer in the succeeding verse (v. 6) which says that two tribes (the tribes of Levi and of Benjamin) were not included in this report and the reason for exclusion is also given in the same verse.[3]

---

[2] Robert Jamieson, David Brown, and A.R. Fausset, *A Commentary on the Old and New Testaments.* (Peabody: Hendrickson Publishers, 1997). Notes on 2 Samuel 24:9

[3] Ibid.

Alleged Contradiction # 4

4. God sent his prophet to threaten David with how many years of famine?
   (a) Seven (2 Samuel 24:13)
   (b) Three (1 Chron. 21:12)

Answer:

There are a number of explanations from different Bible commentators' observations to reconcile this apparent contradiction. These explanations center on the fact that three years of famine had been given to Israel as punishment in David's time previous to this (2 Sam 21:1). With the current year also suffering bad harvest, David is offered another 3 years of famine, thus making them 7 years total.[4]

Here is another explanation for this seeming contradiction. Our many manuscripts copied from the original writing of the prophet Samuel (in Hebrew) and including the ancient translations of the Old Testament (in Greek, Syriac and Arabic) have either "seven" or "three." That's why some translations like the New International Version and the New Living Translation have "three" instead of "seven" for 2 Sam. 24:13, thus eliminating the seeming contradiction. "Three" is more consistent with the two other options God offered King David as punishment for taking census of his fighting men – three months of fleeing from his enemies or three days of plague.[5] Another Bible expositor says, "In the copying of the manuscripts by Jewish scribes, an understandable mistake could have happened here because of the similarity of these

---

[4] Ibid. Notes on 2 Sam. 24:13

[5] Albert Barnes, *Barnes Notes on the Old and New Testaments (Fourteen volumes) 19th Edition*. (Ada, Michigan: Baker Publishing Group, 1983). Notes on 2 Samuel 24:13

two words in Hebrew. A learned writer thinks it a mistake of the copier, writing ז, "seven", for ג, "three."[6]

---

[6] John Gill, *Exposition of the Entire Bible*. (Seattle, Washington: Amazon Digital Services LLC, August 2, 2012). Notes on 2 Sam. 24:13

Alleged Contradiction # 5

5. How old was Ahaziah when he began to rule over Jerusalem?
   (a) Twenty-two (2 Kings 8:26)
   (b) Forty-two (2 Chron. 22:2)

Answer:

From John Gill's Exposition of the Entire Bible, we read this commentary on this supposed contradiction: "it seems best to acknowledge a mistake of the copier, which might easily be made through a similarity of the numeral letters, במ, forty two, for כב, twenty two (d); and the rather since some copies of the Septuagint, and the Syriac and Arabic versions, read twenty two, as in Kings; particularly the Syriac version, used in the church of Antioch from the most early times; a copy of which Bishop Usher obtained at a very great price, and in which the number is twenty two, as he assures us; and that the difficulty here is owing to the carelessness of the transcribers is owned by Glassius (e), a warm advocate for the integrity of the Hebrew text, and so by Vitringa (f): and indeed it is more to the honour of the sacred Scriptures to acknowledge here and there a mistake in the copiers, especially in the historical books, where there is sometimes a strange difference of names and numbers, than to give in to wild and distorted interpretations of them…"[7] NOTE: Christians believe in the inerrancy of the Holy Bible as God inspired the writing of the original manuscripts when written by about 40 different writers living in different times and in different locations. No claim is made that the many copiers making copies from the original manuscripts or copiers of the copies of the original manuscripts did not commit any mistake in their copying. The good translations of the Bible today would carefully compare the thousands of copies of the original manuscripts of

---

[7] Ibid. Notes on 2 Chron. 22:2

the Hebrew and Greek texts as well as the ancient translations of the Bible into other languages such as the Old Testament in Greek and translations to Syriac and Arabic.

Alleged Contradiction # 6

6. How old was Jehoiachin when he began to rule over Jerusalem?
   (a) Eighteen (2 Kings 24:8)
   (b) Eight (2 Chronicles 36:9)

Answer:

We have a comment on this question before starting to explain the Alleged Contradiction. The King James Version, the New King James Version and the New American Standard Bible have "eight" as the age of Jehoiachin when he began to reign for 2 Chronicles 36:9. Many newer Bible translations, though (like New International Version, New Living Translation, and the New English Translation), have "eighteen" in their translations of this same verse. In these Bible versions, there is no contradiction. So the question should really be: Why do some Bible translations put Jehoiachin's age at his accession to the throne as eight and other translations, especially the newer ones, as eighteen. Let us explain the discrepancy of this verse as appears in Bible translations.

According to Keil and Delitzsch, Jehoiachin's age at his accession to the throne is given as eight years in the LXX (short for Septuagint, the Greek translation of the Old Testament) and the Vulgate (Translation to Latin by St Jerome of the Roman Catholic Church). But many manuscripts in Hebrew, Syriac, Arabic and also manuscripts of the LXX have eighteen years in 2 Chronicles 36:9.[8] This tells us that the main references of some English Bible translations having "eight" are from those that are translations themselves (LXX and Vulgate). The references for translating it as "eighteen" are mainly from the Hebrew manuscripts (the original

---

[8] Johann Keil and Franz Delitzsch, *Keil & Delitzsch Commentary of the Old Testament*. (Peabody, MA: Hendrickson Publishers, 1996). Notes on 2 Chron. 36:9-10

language where the Old Testament was written) as well as from Syriac and Arabic manuscripts which are older translations compared to the LXX and Vulgate translations.

R.A. Torrey says 'eighteen years' "is no doubt the genuine reading."[9] Another Bible commentary says the rendering of 'eight years' in 2 Chronicles 36:9 is "probably corrupt for *eighteen*."[10]

[9] R A Torrey, *Treasury of Scripture Knowledge*. (Peabody: Hendrickson Publishers, 2002). Notes on 2 Chron. 36:9

[10] Herbert Edward Ryle, *The Cambridge Bible for Schools and Colleges*. (Charleston, SC: BiblioBazaar, 2009). Notes on 2 Chron. 36:9

Alleged Contradiction # 7

7. How long did he (Jechoiachin) rule over Jerusalem?
    (a) Three months (2 Kings 24:8)
    (b) Three months and ten days (2 Chronicles 36:9)

Answer:

We've already seen above that there's a copyist error in 2 Chronicles 36:9 in some manuscripts. The Cambridge Bible for Schools and Colleges suggests that the clause "and ten days" is a "misplaced fragment of an "original reading *ben shĕmôneh esreh shanah*, i.e. "eighteen years old." So, the "ten days" in this verse must be the ten years to add to the eight years to make Jehoiachin's eighteen years of reign as written in other Hebrew manuscripts, and in the Old Testament translations to Greek, Syriac and Arabic.[11]

---

[11] Ibid.

Alleged Contradiction # 8

8. The chief of the mighty men of David lifted up his spear and killed how many men at one time?
    (a) Eight hundred (2 Samuel 23:8)
    (b) Three hundred (1 Chronicles 11:11)

Answer:

The Bible Knowledge Commentary has this explanation: "Jashobeam, **chief of the officers** (or "chief of 30" ... was famous for slaying **300** at once (1Ch 11:11). 2Sa 23:8 has 800. The difference may be due to a scribal error in copying Chronicles for the Hebrew numerical symbols 300 and 800 look much alike."[12] *The Pulpit Commentary* gives some reasons why 2 Samuel 23:8 is "extremely corrupt."[13] Commenting on the 800, MacArthur says that this is "probably a textual error" and make 300 as the "likely number."[14] This kind of error relates to the mechanical skill of the copyists and has no impact on the biblical teachings or moral lessons that God wants us to know or understand and live by. Continuous research and discoveries especially in the field of archaeology by those who love the integrity of the Scriptures will someday yield more explanations to this issue. As we know, new discoveries in archaeology keep on confirming the Bible records. As we have said in the answer to Alleged Contradiction # 5, God inspired the Biblical writers in writing the original manuscripts but not the many zealous copyists. God is challenging

---

[12] John F. Walvoord (Editor) and Roy B. Zuck (Editor), *The Bible Knowledge Commentary (Old Testament).* (Wheaton, IL: Victor Books, 1985). Notes on 1 Chron. 11:11

[13] Spence and Exell, *The Pulpit Commentary,* Notes on 2 Sam. 23:8.

[14] John MacArthur (author), *The MacArthur Bible Commentary*. (Nashville, Tennessee: Thomas Nelson publisher, 2005). Notes on 2 Sam. 23:8

His people to continue searching, discovering and investigating available data and new discoveries to get what the original writers wrote. Or the right number between these two verses could already have been ascertained but not known yet to this writer.

Alleged Contradiction # 9

9. When did David bring the Ark of the Covenant to Jerusalem? Before defeating the Philistines or after?
   (a) After (2 Samuel 5 and 6)
   (b) Before (1 Chronicles 13 and 14)

Answer:

From the Believer's Bible Commentary, we read this: "The events in chapter 6 did not take place immediately after those recorded in chapter 5. Second Samuel does not always follow a strict chronological order."[15]

The writer(s) or compiler(s) of the Books of Samuel is not known. The prophet Samuel may have written a book (1 Chronicles 29:29 which also mentions other writers) but for sure he could not have written the portions of 1 Samuel 25:1 that records about his death, the chapters following, and also the book of 2 Samuel. Compilation of records of events that happened long time ago, does not necessarily intend to record them in chronological order. But the events are all true. As an example to this, we find in Genesis chapter one the six days when God created what we have on earth today. Then He rested on the seventh day. In chapter two, after mentioning about the seventh day when God rested (2: 2,3), we find again man created in 2: 7. The modern day man may ask, "Was man created before or after God rested?" Compilation of records during Old Testament days did not necessarily follow chronological order.

---

[15] William MacDonald (Author), Arthur L Farstad (Editor), *Believer's Bible Commentary*. (Nashville, Tennessee: Thomas Nelson, 1995). Notes on 2 Samuel 6:1-23

Alleged Contradiction # 10

10. How many pairs of clean animals did God tell Noah to take into the Ark?
    (a) Two (Genesis 6:19, 20)
    (b) Seven (Genesis 7:2). But despite this last instruction only two pairs went into the ark (Genesis 7:8-9)

Answer:

Before answering the Alleged Contradiction in the Bible above, let us first clarify it. Gen. 7:9 says, "They entered the boat in pairs, male and female, just as God had commanded Noah." This does not say "two pairs" but that the animals entered "by pairs." Also, Genesis 6:18, 20 does not say "two" pairs, but a pair, male and female. So, let us understand the question as: Were there two, or seven of each kind of animals (male and female of each kind)?

From *Thru the Bible Commentary*, we read this story: "This was the basis of a lawsuit years ago against Dr. Harry Rimmer who had offered a thousand dollars to anyone who could show a contradiction in the Bible. There were several liberal theologians who testified in a court of law that this was a contradiction. Why would it first say two of each kind and now seven of each kind? Of course, Dr. Rimmer won the lawsuit. All you have to do is turn over to see that when Noah got out of the ark, he offered clean beasts as sacrifices. Where would he have gotten the clean beasts if he had not taken more than two? It was only of the clean beasts that he took seven, and now we know why. Those that were not clean went in by twos, a male and a female."[16]

---

[16] J Vernon McGee (Author), *Thru the Bible, 5 Volumes.* (Nashville, Tennessee: Thomas Nelson publisher, 1990). Notes on Genesis 7:2-3

Alleged Contradiction # 11

11. When David defeated the King of Zobah, how many horsemen did he capture?
    (a) One thousand and seven hundred (2 Samuel 8:4)
    (b) Seven thousand (1 Chronicles 18 :4)

Answer:

Bible translations all agree on 7,000 horsemen or charioteers for 1 Chronicles 18:4. For 2 Samuel 8:4, most translations have 1700, including the King James Version and New King James Version which writes the word "chariots" in italics indicating that it is not in the original language but only supplied by the translators for purpose of clarity. The commentary by Jamieson, Fausset and Brown has this comment: "This great discrepancy in the text of the two narratives seems to have originated with a transcriber in confounding the two Hebrew letters which indicate the numbers, and in neglecting to mark or obscure the points over one of them."[17]

The New International Version and the New Living Translation, however, has 2 Samuel 8:4 as "7000" charioteers making it the same as in 1 Chronicles 18:4. The translators of these versions base their translation from the Greek translation of the Hebrew Old Testament done between two to three centuries before the Christian Era. This Greek translation (called LXX) has "seven thousand" as its translation in this particular verse.[18] This tells us that the Hebrew Old Testament manuscript from

---

[17] Robert Jamieson, A.R. Fausset and David Brown, *Jamieson, Fausset, and Brown's Commentary on the Whole Bible.* (Grand Rapids, MI: Zondervan Publishers, 1999). Notes on 1 Chron. 18:4-8

[18] Biblical Studies Press (author), *NET Bible Full Notes Edition.* (Richardson, Texas: Biblical Studies Press, LLC, 2006). Notes on 2 Sam. 8:4

which the LXX was translated from had 7,000 in 2 Samuel 8:4 as its text making no contradiction with 1 Chronicles 18:4.

Alleged Contradiction # 12

12. How many stalls for horses did Solomon have?
    (a) Forty thousand (1Kings 4:26)
    (b) Four thousand (2 Chronicles 9:25)

Answer:

From the *Big Book of Bible Difficulties* we read this: "This is undoubtedly a copyist error. The ratio of 4,000 horses to 1,400 chariots, as found in the 2 Chronicles passage, is much more reasonable than a ratio of 40,000 to 1,400 found in the 1 Kings text. In the Hebrew language, the visual difference between the two numbers is very slight. The consonants for the number 40 are *rbym*, while the consonants for the number 4 are *rbh* (the vowels were not written in the text in older Hebrew writings). The manuscripts from which the scribe worked may have been smudged or damaged and have given the appearance of being forty thousand rather than four thousand."[19] Newer translations like the New Living Translation, New International Version and the New English Translation have 4,000 for 1 Kings 4:26 instead of 40,000.

John Gill has this to say: "In 2Ch_9:25; it is only four thousand; and therefore some think that here is a mistake of the copier, of "arbaim", forty, for "arbah", four; which it is thought might be through divine permission, in such lesser matters, without any prejudice to the authority of the Scriptures in matters of faith and practice."[20]

Let me give a further clarification of the above. The old Hebrew language wrote their words with only consonants. When read, the readers

---

[19] Norman L. Geissler and Thomas Howe, *The Big Book of Bible Difficulties.* (Grand Rapids, Michigan: Baker Books, 1992). 181

[20] Gill, *Exposition of the Entire Bible,* Notes on 1 Kings 4:26.

pronounced the vowels. As an example in English, a word for "bad" and "bed" would be written the same way, that is, "bd.". According to the context of the sentence or paragraph, the reader would read it either "bad" or "bed." To make the reading easier, modern way of writing the Hebrew words now includes the vowels which were invented for this purpose. This explains the reason why the paragraph above from *The Big Book of Bible Difficulties* and that on Gill following it write the Hebrew words differently, the first one without vowels and the next one with vowels.

Alleged Contradiction # 13

13. In what year of King Asa's reign did Baasha, King of Israel die?
    (a) Twenty-sixth year (1Kings 15:33-16:8)
    (b) Still alive in the thirty-sixth year (2 Chronicles 16:1)

Answer:

"Thirty-sixth year" is a copyist error and would be better written as "sixteenth year," which would be 10 years before Baasha's death. Geisler and Howe in their book say that "The number 'thirty-six' is undoubtedly a copyist error. The actual number was probably 'sixteen.' This error is explained by the fact that the numbers were probably written in numerical notation. In this type of notation, the difference between the letter representing the number 10 xx and the letter representing the number 30 xx was only two small strokes at the top of the letter. It is quite possible that a copyist missed the original and wrote the wrong letter for the number, possibly as the result of a smudged or damaged manuscript at his disposal."[21] This means that instead of "six and ten" (16) what was written in the copying of the manuscript was "six and thirty" (36).

Keil and Delitzsch have a similar comment on this: "the letters ל (30) and י (10), which are somewhat similar in the ancient Hebrew characters, having been interchanged by a copyist."[22] When one writes the character for ten a little bit bigger, it could look like the character for thirty. And then if that part of the papyrus or parchment is partly damaged, the characters would not be clear to the copyist.

---

[21] Geisser and Howe, *The Big Book of Bible Difficulties*, 209.

[22] Keil and Delitzch, *Keil & Delitzsch Commentary of the Old Testament*, Notes on 2 Chron. 16:1-5.

The original manuscripts written by the original writers of the Bible passed through many hands as they were being copied again and again by many copyists. When the original manuscripts were damaged or lost, copyists had to copy from copies of the original writings. As generations went by, copyists could be copying from copies of the original manuscripts or copies of copies of the original writings. And then even the copies or copies of copies of the original manuscripts themselves would wear out or be damaged by constant copying of the many copyists. The writers of the original manuscripts were inspired by God when they wrote the Scriptures. But no claim is made that the copies or copies of copies of the original manuscripts are inspired by God. Human error could take place. The variance in characters or the spelling of words do not alter the meaning of the sentence or paragraph and, therefore, do not affect doctrines or teachings of the Christian faith. Also, there are thousands of copies of manuscripts of the Scriptures in different museums of the world. For all copyists to make the same mistake of copying on the same word is most unlikely. Therefore, by comparing all available manuscripts, plus considering the many translations of the Bible to different earlier languages, make us feel confident of the authenticity of the Bible we presently have. In fact, someone said that even if we destroy all the Bibles in the world today, and go back to the thousands of manuscripts available in various repositories in the world, we will still come up with the same Bible versions today. "It is reassuring to remember that when the Lord Jesus was on earth, He used an edition of the OT (not the original manuscripts) and He quoted this text as the Word of God. We can use reputable versions of the Bible today with the same confidence that they are the Word of God."[23]

---

[23] William MacDonald and Arthur L. Farstad, *Believer's Bible Commentary.* (Nashville, Tennessee: Thomas Nelson publisher, 1995). Notes on 2 Chron. 2:1-18

Alleged Contradiction # 14

14. How many overseers did Solomon appoint for the work of building the temple?
    (a) Three thousand six hundred (2 Chronicles 2:2)
    (b) Three thousand three hundred (1 Kings 5:16)

Answer:

Though the number of overseers in the two accounts above are not the same, "the sum-total of the overseers is the same in both accounts (3300 + 550 = 3850 in the books of Kings, and 3600 + 250 = 3850 in the Chronicles); and we must therefore follow J. H. Michaelis, and explain the differences as resulting from a different method of classification, namely, from the fact that in the Chronicles, the Canaanitish overseers are distinguished from the Israelitish (viz., 3600 Canaanites and 250 Israelites), whereas in the books of Kings the *inferiores et superiores praefecti* are distinguished... and that in the 3300 of our chapter the superintendents of Canaanitish descent are not included.[24] Barnes explains it this way: "Comparing this verse and 1Ki_9:23 with 2Ch_2:18; 2Ch_8:10, the entire number of the overseers will be seen to be stated by both writers at 3,850; but in the one case nationality, in the other degree of authority, is made the principle of the division."[25]

---

[24] Keil and Delitzch, *Keil & Delitzsch Commentary of the Old Testament*, Notes on 1 Kings 5:16.

[25] Albert Barnes, *Barnes Notes on the Old and New Testaments,* Notes on 1 Kings 5:16.

Alleged Contradiction # 15

15. Solomon built a facility containing how many baths?
    (a) Two thousand (1 Kings 7:26)
    (b) Over three thousand (2 Chronicles 4:5)

Answer:

A bath was a Hebrew measure for liquids containing about eight gallon and three quarts.[26] This water was used in the Jewish temple to clean the animals the temple priests killed, cut and offered as religious sacrifices. It was also used by the priests in cleaning up themselves related to their temple services.

1 Kings 7:26 says that the basin (called "The Sea") in the temple contains two thousand baths while 2 Chronicles 4:5 says three thousand. Adam Clarke explains the seeming discrepancy this way as his comments on the Chronicles records: "In 1Ki 7:26, it is said to hold only two thousand baths. As this book was written after the Babylonish captivity, it is very possible that reference is here made to the Babylonish bath which might have been less than the Jewish. We have already seen that the cubit of Moses, or of the ancient Hebrews, was longer than the Babylonish by one palm; see on 2Ch 3:3 (note). It might be the same with the measures of capacity; so that two thousand of the ancient Jewish baths might have been equal to three thousand of those used after the captivity. The Targum cuts the knot by saying, 'It received three thousand baths of dry measure, and held two thousand of liquid measure.'"[27] (Note: Targum is an ancient Aramaic paraphrase or interpretation of

---

[26] Orville J Nave, *Nave's Topical Bible*. (Nashville, Tennessee: Southwestern Company, 1962). Notes on topic "bath"

[27] Adam Clarke, *Adam Clarke's Commentary on the Bible*. (Nashville, Tennessee: Thomas Nelson publisher, 1997). Notes on 2 Chron. 4:5

the Hebrew Bible made from about the first century before the Christian Era. It was used in the synagogues and also in Biblical instruction at a time in Jewish history when most people had Aramaic as the common language of communication.)

Alleged Contradictions # 16 to # 23.

These Alleged Contradictions #16 to #23 (eight items) will be answered with one explanation because they refer to the same passages in Ezra (2:1-67) and Nehemiah (7:6-69). First, let's get to some background information about Ezra and Nehemiah. The nation of Israel was in exile during the Babylonian Empire. When the Persian Empire replaced the Babylonian Empire, King Cyrus, its first king, ordered the reconstruction of the temple in Jerusalem and encouraged the Jews to go back to their native land and rebuild the temple. Ezra made a list of the people who returned to Jerusalem. After the temple was rebuilt, the next project to be done was the rebuilding of the walls of Jerusalem to protect the people living there. After receiving a report that the walls were not yet rebuilt, Nehemiah asked leave from the Persian king, whom he served as cupbearer to go to Jerusalem and help build the walls. In the book Nehemiah wrote and bears his name, he also made a list of the people who came to Jerusalem from exile. This is where we find the alleged discrepancies. The writer of "*101 Contradictions in the Bible*" listed eight errors in comparing the list of Ezra from that of Nehemiah. Actually, there are fourteen instances where the figures differ.

16. Of the Israelites who were freed from the Babylonian captivity, how many were the children of Pahrath-Moab?
    (a) Two thousand eight hundred and twelve (Ezra 2:6)
    (b) Two thousand eight hundred and eighteen (Nehemiah 7:11)

17. How many were the children of Zattu?
    (a) Nine hundred and forty-five (Ezra 2:8)
    (b) Eight hundred and forty-five (Nehemiah 7:13)

18. How many were the children of Azgad?
    (a) One thousand two hundred and twenty-two (Ezra 2:12)

     (b) Two thousand three hundred and twenty-two (Nehemiah 7:17)

19. How many were the children of Adin?
     (a) Four hundred and fifty-four (Ezra 2:5)
     (b) Six hundred and fifty-five (Nehemiah 7:20)

20. How many were the children of Hashum?
     (a) Two hundred and twenty-three (Ezra 2:19)
     (b) Three hundred and twenty-eight (Nehemiah 7 :22)

21. How many were the children of Bethel and Ai?
     (a) Two hundred and twenty-three (Ezra 2:28)
     (b) One hundred and twenty-three (Nehemiah 7:32)

22. Ezra 2:64 and Nehemiah 7:66 agree that the total number of the whole assembly was 42,360. Yet the numbers do not add up to anything close. The totals obtained from each book is as follows:
     (a) 29,818 (Ezra)
     (b) 32,089 (Nehemiah)

23. How many singers accompanied the assembly?
     (a) Two hundred (Ezra 2:65)
     (b) Two hundred and forty-five (Nehemiah 7:67)

Answer:

Geisler and Howe offer this solution:

"First, it is possible that each of these is a copyist error. One of the most problematic areas of transcription for the Jewish scribe was copying numbers. It is certainly conceivable that out of these rather large lists of names and numbers there would be a number of copyist errors.

"Second, it is also possible that Ezra and Nehemiah compiled their lists at different times. Ezra may have compiled a list of those who left Babylon with Zerubbabel, while Nehemiah compiled his list of those who actually made it to Jerusalem. In some cases, people who left Babylon with the intention of going back to rebuild Jerusalem may have turned back or died along the way. In other cases, family members in other lands got word of the migration and rendezvoused with their relatives along the way from Babylon to Jerusalem."[28]

---

[28] Geisser and Howe, *The Big Book of Bible Difficulties*, 214.

Alleged Contradiction # 24

24. What was the name of King Abijah's mother?
    (a) Michaiah, daughter of Uriel of Gibeah (2 Chronicles 13:2)
    (b) Maachah, daughter of Absalom (2 Chronicles 11:20). But Absalom had only one daughter whose name was Tamar (2 Samuel 14:27)

Answer:

To understand the question above, let me explain that Michaiah and Maachah are the same person. Uriel of Gibeah and Absalom refer also to the same person. We get this explanation from Clarke who says that the Targum gives the following reason why the names refer to the same persons: "Abijah reigned three years in Jerusalem; and his mother's name was Michaiah, daughter of Uriel of Gibeatha. She is the same as Michah, the daughter of Absalom; but, because she was an upright woman, her name was changed into the more excellent name Michaiah, and her father's name into that of Uriel of Gibeatha, that the name of Absalom might not be remembered."[29]

On the issue that Absalom had only one daughter whose name was Tamar (2 Samuel 14:27), we have this explanation from *The Pulpit Commentary*: "As in our note (2Ch 11:20), the word "daughter," as in many similar cases, stands for granddaughter. Thus the father of Maachah was Uriel of Gibeah, and her mother Tamar, daughter of Absalom. Josephus ('Ant., '8.10. § 1) proffers us this connecting link of explanation."[30] (Note: Josephus was a Jewish historian who lived during the first century of the Christian Era.)

---

[29] Clarke, *Adam Clarke's Commentary on the Bible*, Notes on 2 Chron. 11:20.

[30] Spence and Exell, *The Pulpit Commentary,* Notes on 2 Chron. 13:1-22.

Alleged Contradiction # 25

25. Did Joshua and the Israelites capture Jerusalem?
    (a) Yes (Joshua 10:23, 40)
    (b) No (Joshua 15:63)

Answer:

Joshua 10: 40 indeed says that "Joshua conquered all the land." And yet in Joshua 15:63, it says that "As for the Jebusites, the inhabitants of Jerusalem, the children of Judah could not drive them out; but the Jebusites dwell with the children of Judah." A Bible commentary gives this explanation on Joshua 10:40: "The cities that have been described in this passage are all in the southern hill country and the southern Shephelah. Cities such as Gezer and Jerusalem are not mentioned as being attacked. The description given in the verse circumscribes this region. Since the kings who controlled the region had been defeated, the territory was now considered to belong to the Israelites. The use of hyperbole in describing the total nature of the destruction is common in conquest accounts. The text itself demonstrates that it is hyperbole in Jos_ 15:13-16, where inhabitants of Hebron and Debir are mentioned. This type of hyperbole is used in reference to Israel in the Merenptah Inscription, where it is claimed that there are no descendants of Israel remaining, and in the Mesha Inscription, where Israel is described as utterly perished forever. Such statements are the rhetoric indicative of military victory and can be found in Hittite, Egyptian and Assyrian accounts of campaigns. This does not suggest the account is inaccurate, deceptive or misleading, for any reader would have recognized this well-known rhetorical style for reporting the results of battle."[31]

---

[31] John H Walton, Victor H. Matthews and Mark W. Chavalas. *The IVP Bible Background Commentary: Old Testament.* (Downers Grove, IL: IVP Academic, 2000). Notes on Jos. 10: 40

The king of Jerusalem was one of the kings that Joshua captured and killed in Joshua 10:23 in the battle at Makkedah (Joshua 10:15-28). Conquering all these kings in battle would mean having legal authority over all their lands, though the Israelites still had to actually possess many of the places under these kings.

26. Who was the father of Joseph, husband of Mary?
    (a) Jacob (Matthew 1:16)
    (b) Heli (Luke 3:23)

Answer:

Joseph is son of Jacob biologically. Joseph is also son of Heli as a son-in-law, being married to Mary, Heli's daughter. This is why, in answering the next Alleged Contradiction below, we note the two genealogies of Jesus being traced to the same person, David the king of Israel.

Alleged Contradiction # 27

27. Jesus descended from which son of David?
    (a) Solomon (Matthew 1:6)
    (b) Nathan (Luke 3:31)

Answer:

From *The Big Book of Bible Difficulties*, we find that this dissimilarity should be expected, since the genealogies listed are two different lines of ancestors, one traced through His legal father, Joseph and the other through His biological mother, Mary. Matthew gives the official or legal line, since he addressed Jesus' genealogy to Jewish concerns for the Jewish Messiah's credentials which required that the Messiah come from the seed of Abraham and the line of David (cf. Matt. 1:1). Luke, with a broader Greek audience in view addresses himself to their interest in Jesus as the Perfect Man (which was the quest of Greek thought). Thus, he traces Jesus back to the first man, Adam (Luke 3:38).

That Matthew gives Jesus' paternal genealogy and Luke his maternal genealogy is further supported by several facts. First of all, while both lines trace Christ to David, the king of Israel, each genealogy is through a different son of David. Matthew traces Jesus through Joseph (His legal father) to David's son, Solomon the king, by whom Christ rightfully inherited the throne of David (cf. 2 Sam. 7:12ff). Luke's purpose, on the other hand, is to show the genealogy through His biological mother, Mary, through whom He can rightfully claim to be fully human, the redeemer of humanity. Mary is descended from one of King David's son named Nathan (Luke 3:31).

Further, Luke does not say that he is giving Jesus' genealogy through Joseph. Rather, he notes that Jesus was "as was supposed" (Luke 3:23) the son of Joseph, while He was actually, not just supposedly, the son of Mary.

The two genealogies can be summarized as follows:

Solomon and Nathan are both children of King David. Jesus descended from both. Jesus descended from Solomon through Joseph, legal father (kingly genealogy of Israel, as King of Israel). Jesus also descended from Nathan through Mary, human mother of Jesus (human genealogy from Adam as Savior of humanity).[32]

---

[32] Geisser and Howe, *The Big Book of Bible Difficulties*, pp 385-386.

Alleged Contradiction # 28

28. Who was the father of Shealtiel?
    (a) Jechoniah (Matthew 1:12)
    (b) Neri (Luke 3:27)

Answer:

According to the Alexandrian chronicle, Jeconiah is the same person as Neri.[33] The Alexandrian Chronicle is composed of "illuminated fragments" in papyrus which is kept in the Pushkin Museum in Moscow, Russia.[34] Beginning in the deportation of Israel to other nations, many Jews have had two names just like Daniel (also called Belteshazzar), Hananiah (also called Shadrach), Mishael (also called Meshach), and Azariah (also called Abed-nego) (Dan. 1:7). Even in the New Testament times, Peter is also called Cephas and Matthew is called Levi (Matt. 10:2-3; Luke 5:27).

---

[33] Gill, *Exposition of the Entire Bible,* Notes on Matt. 1:12.

[34] Oxford Reference, "Alexandrian World Chronicle." Available from http://www.oxfordreference.com/view/10.1093/oi/authority.20110803095401732. Internet; (accessed 20 December 2016)

29. Which son of Zerubbabel was an ancestor of Jesus Christ?
    (a) Abiud (Matthew 1:13)
    (b) Rhesa (Luke 3:27) but the seven sons Zerubbabel are as follows: i. Mesullam, ii. Hanahiah, iii. Hashubad, iv. Ohel, v. Berechiah, vi. Hasadiah, vii. Jushabhesed (I Chronicles 3:19,20). The names of Abiud and Rhesa do not fit in anyway.

Answer:

Rhesa (*rosh*) is not a person but a title of Zerubbabel meaning "prince" which precedes the name "Zerubbabel."[35] Abiud, on the other hand, could be another name for Zerubbabel's son as explained by Gill: "The children of Zorobabel are said in 1Ch 3:19, to be Meshullam, and Hananiah, and Shelomith their sister, but no mention is made of Abiud: he seems to be the same with Meshullam the eldest son, who might have two names; nor is this unlikely, since it was usual, especially about the time of the Babylonish captivity, for men to have more names than one, as may be observed in Daniel and others, Dan 1:7 where they went by one, and in Judea by another."[36]

---

[35] A. R Fausset, *Fausset's Bible Dictionary.* (Grand Rapids, MI: Zondervan Publishers, 1949). Entry on Rhesa

[36] Gill, *Exposition of the Entire Bible,* Notes on Matt. 1:13-15.

Alleged Contradiction # 30

30. Who was the father of Uzziah?
    (a) Joram (Matthew 1:8)
    (b) Amaziah (2 Chronicles 26:1)

Answer:

Here is an explanation to this Alleged Contradiction from Geisser and Howe:

"Ahaziah was apparently the immediate son of Joram, and Uzziah was a distant "son" (descendant). Just as the word "son" in the Bible also means grandson, even so the term "begot" means "became the ancestor of," and the one "begotten" is "the descendant of."

Matthew, therefore, is not giving a complete chronology, but an abbreviated genealogy of Christ's ancestry. A comparison of Matthew 1:8 and 1 Chronicles 3:11-12 reveals the three generations between Joram and Uzziah (Azariah);

MATTHEW 1:8	CHRONICLES 3:11-12
Joram	Joram
....	Ahaziah
....	Joash
....	Amaziah
Uzziah	Uzziah Uzziah (also called Azariah)"[37]

36

The *A Popular Commentary of the New Testament* confirms this and gives the reason:

"Between **Joram** and **Uzziah,** three names are intentionally omitted: Ahaziah, Joash, and Amaziah, probably to reduce the number of generations. These three were chosen, either because personally unworthy, or because descendants to the fourth generation from Jezebel, through Athaliah.[38]

Further explanation from *The Pulpit Commentary* makes the issue at hand even clearer:

"It is not likely that St. Matthew omitted them, but that they were absent from the form which he used. If we seek for a reason why these precise names are omitted, we may probably find it in the fact of their being descended from Jezebel; while the language of the second commandment would suggest that to the fourth generation the children' of that race would suffer for the sins of their parents. To the Jewish compiler of this genealogy no argument more forcible for the removal of these names could have been suggested. It will be seen that the word "begat" in these verses does not signify always the direct succession of son to father."[39]

The Bible verse that comes to my mind to support the argument above is Deut. 34: 7 – "maintaining love to thousands, and forgiving wickedness, rebellion and sin. Yet he does not leave the guilty unpunished; he punishes the children and their children for the sin of the parents to the third and fourth generation." (NIV)

---

[37] Geisser and Howe, *The Big Book of Bible Difficulties*, pp 325.

[38] Philip Schaff (Editor), *A Popular Commentary of the New Testament*. (New York: Charles Scribner's Sons, 1960). Notes on Matt. 1:8

[39] Spence and Exell, *The Pulpit Commentary,* Notes on Matt. 1:8.

Alleged Contradiction # 31

31. Who was the father of Jechoniah?
    (a) Josiah (Matthew 1:11)
    (b) Jehoiakim (I Chronicles 3:16)

Answer:

Before we explain the answer to this question, to readers who would actually read their Bibles on this issue, let us bring about the fact that some translations like the NIV and the NLT do not use the word "Jechoniah" but "Jehoiachin." Most of the rest use "Jechoniah." The NET Bible explains that the Hebrew word Jechoniah is a variation of Jehoiachin.[40] This is the reason why the Amplified Bible in 1 Chronicles 3:16 writes in parenthesis the word "Jechoniah" after the word Jehoiachin. Also, that Jehoiachin is not to be confused with the name of his father, Jehoiakim.

Let us now state the Alleged Contradiction more clearly: In 1 Chronicles 3:16 the father of Jechoniah or Jehoiachin is Jehoiakim while in Matthew 1:11, the father of Jechoniah (Jehoiachin) is Josiah.

In the complete genealogy in 1 Chronicles, Josiah is the father of Jehoiakim and Jehoiakim is the father of Jehoiachin or Jechoniah. Josiah, therefore, is the grandfather, not the father of Jehoiachin (Jechoniah) as stated in Matthew 1:11. The NET Bible explains that Matthew is "selective in his genealogy for a theological purpose."[41] The *Popular Commentary on the New Testament* gives another reason for omitting the name of Jehoiakim in the genealogy copied by Matthew by saying

---

[40] Biblical Studies Press (author), *NET Bible Full Notes Edition*, Notes on 1 Chron. 3:16.

[41] Biblical Studies Press (author), *NET Bible Full Notes Edition*, Notes on Matt 1:11.

that Jehoiakim "was forcefully placed on the throne by the king of Egypt, hence unworthy of mention"[42]

---

[42] Schaff (Editor), *A Popular Commentary of the New Testament*, Notes on Matt. 1:11.

Alleged Contradiction # 32

32. How many generations were there from the Babylonian exile until Christ?
    (a) Matthew says fourteen (Matthew 1:17)
    (b) But a careful count of the generations reveals only thirteen (see Matthew 1:12-16)

Answer:

Albert Barnes gives a very satisfying answer to this Alleged Contradiction. He says:

"This division of the names in the genealogical tables was doubtless adopted for the purpose of aiding the memory. It was common among the Jews; and other similar instances are preserved. The Jews were destitute of books besides the Old Testament, and they had but few copies of that among them, and those chiefly in their synagogues. They would therefore naturally devise plans to keep up the remembrance of the principal facts in their history. One method of doing this was to divide the tables of genealogy into portions of equal length, to be committed to memory. This greatly facilitated the remembrance of the names. A man who wished to commit to memory the names of a regiment of soldiers would naturally divide it into companies and platoons, and this would greatly facilitate his work. This was doubtless the reason in the case before us. And, though it is not strictly accurate, yet it was the Jewish way of keeping their records, and answered their purpose. There were three leading persons and events that nearly, or quite, divided their history into equal portions: Abraham, David, and the Babylonian captivity. From one to the other was about 14 generations, and by omitting a few names it was sufficiently accurate to be made a general guide or directory in recalling the principal events in their history.

"In counting these divisions, however, it will be seen that there is some difficulty in making out the number 14 in each division. This may be explained in the following manner: In the first division, Abraham is the first and David the last, making 14 altogether. In the second series, David would naturally be placed first, and the 14 was completed in Josiah, about the time of the captivity, as sufficiently near for the purpose of convenient computation, 2 Chr. 35. In the third division Josiah would naturally be placed first, and the number was completed in Joseph; so that David and Josiah would be reckoned twice. This may be shown by the following table of the names:

First Division	Second Division	Third Division
Abraham	David	Josias
Isaac	Solomon	Jechonias
Jacob	Roboam	Salathiel
Judas	Abia	Zorobabel
Phares	Asa	Abiud
Esrom	Josaphat	Eliakim
Aram	Joram	Azor
Aminadab	Ozias	Sadoc
Naasson	Joatham	Achim
Salmon	Achaz	Eliud
Boaz	Ezekias	Eleazar
Obed	Manasses	Matthan
Jesse	Amon	Jacob
David	Josias	Joseph
14	14	14

[43]

The *Bible Knowledge Commentary* (New Testament) says that "Matthew's genealogy answered the important question a Jew would rightfully ask

---

[43] Barnes, *Barnes Notes on the Old and New Testaments,* Notes on Matt. 1:17.

about anyone who claimed to be King of the Jews. Is He a descendant of David through the rightful line of succession? Matthew answered yes!"[44]

Matthew was not for exactness but was following Jewish cultural norms in recalling names and committing them to memory in an age where written documents are not common and very expensive to make.

---

[44] John R. Walvoord (Editor) and Roy B. Zuck, *The Bible Knowledge Commentary-An Exposition of the Scriptures by Dallas Seminary Faculty-New Testament.* (Colorado Springs, CO: Chariot Victor Publishing, 1998). Notes on Matthew 1:2-17

Alleged Contradiction # 33

33. Who was the father of Shelah?
    (a) Cainan (Luke 3:35-36)
    (b) Arphaxad (Genesis 2:12)

Answer:

Three Bible commentators can help us understand this seeming discrepancy. Geisser and Howe say "It is better to view Genesis 5 and 10 as adequate genealogies, not complete chronologies"[45]

Gill says that "Cainan" is in many Greek manuscripts and also in the Latin Vulgate and all the oriental versions. But he explains: "This Cainan is not mentioned by Moses in Gen_11:12 nor has he ever appeared in any Hebrew copy of the Old Testament, nor in the Samaritan version, nor in the Targum; nor is he mentioned by Josephus, nor in 1Ch_1:24 where the genealogy is repeated; nor is it in Beza's most ancient Greek copy of Luke: it indeed stands in the present copies of the Septuagint, but was not originally there; and therefore could not be taken by Luke from thence, but seems to be owing to some early negligent transcriber of Luke's Gospel, and since put into the Septuagint to give it authority:..."[46]

Another Bible commentator offers yet another explanation and an exhortation to Bible readers. He says,

"This Cainan, the son of Arphaxad, and father of Sala, is not found in any other Scripture genealogy. See Gen_10:24; Gen_11:12; 1Ch_1:18, 1Ch_1:24, where Arphaxad is made the father of Sala, and no mention at all made of Cainan. Some suppose that Cainan was a surname of Sala,

---

[45] Geisser and Howe, *The Big Book of Bible Difficulties*, p 36.

[46] Gill, *Exposition of the Entire Bible,* Notes on Luke 3:36.

and that the names should be read together thus, The son of Heber, the son of Salacainan, the son of Arphaxad, etc. If this does not untie the knot, it certainly cuts it; and the reader may pass on without any great scruple or embarrassment."[47]

---

[47] Clarke, *Adam Clarke's Commentary on the Bible*, Notes on Luke 3:36.

34. Was John the Baptist Elijah who was to come?
    (a) Yes (Matthew 11:14, 17:10-13)
    (b) No (John 1:19-21)

Answer:

Jesus indeed say in Matthew 11:14 that John the Baptist was the Elijah that was to come as prophesied in Malachi 4:5. This means that John the Baptist would be "in the spirit and power of Elijah" (Luke 1: 17) and does not mean that John the Baptist is the very Elijah in the Old Testament who came back to life as John the Baptist. Many of the Jews thought that since Elijah was taken up to heaven (2 Kings 2:11) by a chariot and horses of fire, he did not really die and would come back to earth again in bodily form.[48] In answer to the Jews who asked him with this kind of notion, John the Baptist answered them that he was not Elijah (John 1:21). In the Bible the word "heaven" could mean the place where God's throne is (Psalm 11:4). It also means just the sky above us (Gen. 7:23, KJV, AMP). Elijah's going to "heaven" could mean just going up to the sky and, since he requested God that he die and for Him to take his life (1 Kings 19:4), be buried by God somewhere where no man knows just like what happened to Moses (Deut. 34:5,6).

---

[48] Gill, *Exposition of the Entire Bible,* Notes on John 1:21.

Alleged Contradiction # 35

35. Would Jesus inherit David's throne?
    (a) Yes. So said the angel (Luke 1:32)
    (b) No, since he is a descendant of Jehoiakim (see Matthew 1: 11, 1 Chronicles 3:16). And Jehoiakim was cursed by God so that none of his descendants can sit upon David's throne (Jeremiah 36:30)

Answer:

It is true that Jehoiakim was cursed by God so that none of his descendant could sit upon David's throne according to Jeremiah 36:30. The fulfillment of this curse happened when Israel was deported to Babylon (Matt. 1:11) so that no one of Jehoiakim's sons ascended to David's throne. The statement above that Jesus was a descendant of Jehoiakim is to be qualified, though. Jesus is a descendant of Jehoiakim, who is a descendant of King Solomon (Matt. 1:6), David's son, only in the sense of His foster father, Joseph. But Jesus' mother in the flesh, Mary, is a descendant of Nathan (Luke 3:31), another son of King David, thus, making Jesus qualified to inherit King David's throne.

On God's curse on Jehoiakim for doing evil in the sight of God, McGee says this is what exactly happened to this king and that Jesus' "blood title to the throne of David" comes from Mary, his earthly mother, "born in the line of Nathan, another son of David."[49]

---

[49] McGee, *Thru the Bible, 5 Volumes,* Notes on Jer. 36:30.

Alleged Contradiction # 36

36. Jesus rode into Jerusalem on how many animals?
    (a) One – colt (Mark 11:7; cf Luke 19: 35). "And they brought the colt to Jesus and threw their garments on it; and he sat upon it."
    (b) Two – colt and an ass (Matthew 21:7). "They brought the ass and the colt and put their garments on them and he sat thereon."

Answer:

A.T. Robertson, using his knowledge of the Koine Greek grammar, says that "Matthew does not contradict that, referring to the garments (*ta himatia*) put on the colt by "them" (*auton*), not to the two asses ... The garments thrown on the animals were the outer garments (*himatia*)" and that Jesus sat upon the garments on the colt and not the garments upon the two animals.[50] This is why the Amplified Bible explains Jesus sitting on "them" as sitting on the "clothing" and not on the animals. MacArthur says that "Matthew is the only Gospel writer who mentions the mare donkey... The mare was brought along, possibly to induce the colt to cooperate."[51]

---

[50] A.T. Robertson (Author), *Word Pictures in the New Testament (6 Vols.)*. (Ada, Michigan: Baker Publishing Group, 1982). Notes on Matt. 21:7

[51] MacArthur, *The MacArthur Bible Commentary*, Notes on Matt. 21:7.

Alleged Contradiction # 37

37. How did Simon Peter find out that Jesus was the Christ?
    (a) By a revelation from heaven (Matthew 16:17)
    (b) His brother Andrew told him (John 1:41)

Answer:

True believers of Christ have an experience that non-believers do not experience and, therefore, do not understand. True followers of Christ not only hear from men or their leaders but also hear from God Himself. In Acts 17: 11, we find Jews who were considered "more noble" because they not only listen to Paul's teachings but examined the Scriptures to see what God through His Spirit would reveal to them as written there. It is true that Andrew told his brother Simon Peter about Christ (John 1:41). But Peter still had to hear it from God Himself through the Holy Spirit to confirm what his brother told him. And that is what Christ was referring to in Matt. 16:17.

I would like to make an additional explanation and application on this important truth. Our fellow believers or our Christian leaders may tell us that we are children of God based on God's Word and/or based on what they observe in our lives. But it is important that the Holy Spirit Himself "testifies with our spirit that we are children of God" (Rom. 8:16). It is one thing for people to tell us something. It is another thing for God Himself expressing that truth within our hearts through His indwelling Holy Spirit.

Alleged Contradiction # 38

38. Where did Jesus first meet Simon Peter and Andrew?
    (a) By the Sea of Galilee (Matthew 4:18-22)
    (b) On the banks of river Jordan (John 1:42). After that, Jesus decided to go to Galilee (John 1:43)

Answer:

Jesus first met Simon Peter (John 1:41, 42) in "Bethabara beyond the Jordan" where John the Baptist was baptizing (John 1:28). Jesus did not call him that time to follow Him. Later, when Jesus met Simon Peter by the sea of Galilee (Matt. 4:18-22), and that was after the miracle of the large catch of fish, Jesus called him/them (Luke 5:1-11). The Scriptures do not say in either Matt. 4:18-22 or Luke 5:1-11 that this was the first time Jesus ever met Peter.

Alleged Contradiction # 39

39. When Jesus met Jairus was Jairus' daughter already dead?
    (a) Yes. Matthew 9:18 quotes him as saying, "My daughter has just died."
    (b) No. Mark 5:23 quotes him as saying, "My little daughter is at the point of death."

Answer:

Ryle in his Bible commentary on Mark 5:23 says: "The original word here used is one of the frequent Latinisms of St Mark. See Introduction. She lay a dying (Luk_8:42), and all but gone when he left her, the sands of life ebbing out so fast, that he could even say of her that she was "dead" (Mat_9:18), at one moment expressing himself in one language, at the next in another."[52]

On Matt. 9:18 Clarke has this comment: "**My daughter is even now dead** - Or, my daughter was just now dying; αρτι ετελευτησεν, or, is by this time dead: i.e. as Mr. Wakefield properly observes, She was so ill when I left home that she must be dead by this time. This turn of the expression reconciles the account given here with that in Mark and Luke. Michaelis conjectures that, in the Hebrew original, the words must have stood thus, התמ התע atah matah, which, without the points, may signify either, She is dead, or She is dying."[53] (Note: Point system in later Hebrew writing is a way of indicating where a vowel could possibly be present in the Hebrew writing which was originally written with only consonants.)

---

[52] Ryle, *The Cambridge Bible for Schools and Colleges*, Notes on Mark 5:23.

[53] Clarke, *Adam Clarke's Commentary on the Bible*, Notes on Matt. 9:18.

Alleged Contradiction # 40

40. Did Jesus allow his disciples to keep a staff on their journey?
    (a) Yes (Mark 6:8)
    (b) No (Matthew 10:9; Luke 9:3)

Answer:

Geisser and Rowe say: "A closer examination reveals that the account in Mark 6:8 declares that the disciples are to take nothing except a staff, which a traveler would normally have. Whereas the account in Matthew states that they are not to acquire another staff. There is no discrepancy between these texts. Mark's account is saying that they should not take an *extra* staff or tunic. The text reads "Provide neither … two tunics, nor sandals, nor staffs" (plural: vv. 9-10). It does not say that they should not take a staff (singular). So there is no contradiction."[54] In other words, "staff" in Mark is in singular form, while in Matthew it is plural.

From Gill we read: "**nor yet with staves:** that is, with more than one staff, which was sufficient to assist them, and lean upon in journeying: for, according to Mark, one was allowed; as though they might take a travelling staff, yet not staves for defence, or to fight with; see Mat 26:55. Now these several things were forbidden them, partly because they would be burdensome to them in travelling; and partly because they were not to be out any long time, but were quickly to return again; and chiefly to teach them to live and depend upon divine providence."[55]

---

[54] Geisser and Howe, *The Big Book of Bible Difficulties*, p 339.

[55] Gill, *Exposition of the Entire Bible,* Notes on Matt. 10:10.

Alleged Contradiction# 41

41. Did Herod think that Jesus was John the Baptist?
    (a) Yes (Matthew 14:2; Mark 6:16)
    (b) No (Luke 9:9)

Answer:

In answer to this Alleged Contradiction, Baker's *New Testament Commentary* has this explanation:

"Luk_9:7-8. And he was perplexed because by some it was said that John had risen from the dead, by others that Elijah had appeared, and by still others that one of the ancient prophets had come back to life.

a. Some people were convinced that Jesus was John the Baptist restored to life. This may seem somewhat odd, since Scripture nowhere ascribes any miracles to the Baptist. But it is probable that by this group John was held in such high esteem that the ability to perform miracles was attributed to him.

b. Another group said, "Elijah has appeared." Had not Elijah's return, as Messiah's forerunner, been predicted by Malachi (Mal_4:5)? Cf. Isa_40:3; and see above, on Luk_1:76; Luk_7:27 (cf. Mar_1:1-3).

c. The third group, not wishing to be very definite, was convinced, nevertheless, that in the person of Jesus one of the ancient prophets had come back to life. See also on verses Luk_9:18-19.

Luk_9:9. But Herod said, John I beheaded. Who, then, is this man about whom I am hearing such things?

Note that Luke does not report what the tetrarch thought of suggestions (b) and (c). Herod may have reflected on these answers briefly, and then dismissed them from his mind. It would seem that, after some hesitation, he was always coming back to suggestion (a)."[56]

We see here that Herod's statement to his servants that John the Baptist had risen from the dead as recorded in Matthew and Mark did not originate with him. He heard of three suggestions (Luke 9:7-8). Luke's account did not say which one Herod finally thought who Jesus was. But Matthew and Mark did.

---

[56] William Hendriksen (Author) and Simon J. Kistemaker (Author), *New Testament Commentary Set*, 12 Volumes. (Ada, Michigan: Baker Academic of Baker Publishing Group, 2002). Notes on Luke 9:-7-9

Alleged Contradiction # 42

42. Did John the Baptist recognize Jesus before his baptism?
    (a) Yes (Matthew 3:13-14)
    (b) No (John 1:32,33)

Answer:

From Geisser and Rowe, we read this explanation: "John may have known Jesus before His baptism only by *reputation,* not by *recognition.* Or, he may have known Jesus only by *personal acquaintance*, but not by *divine manifestation*. After all, Jesus and John were relatives (Luke 1: 36), even though they were reared in different places (Luke 1:80; 2:51). However, even though John may have had some previous family contact with Jesus, He had never known Jesus as He was revealed at His baptism when the Spirit descended on Him and the Father spoke from heaven (Matt. 3:16-17). The context indicates that, up to His baptism, no one really knew Jesus as He would then "be revealed to Israel" (John 1:31)."[57]

---

[57] Geisser and Howe, *The Big Book of Bible Difficulties*, pp 404-405.

Alleged Contradiction # 43

43. Did John the Baptist recognize Jesus after his baptism?
    (a) Yes (John 1:32, 33)
    (b) No (Matthew 11:2)

Answer:

At the time of Christ, many Jews just like John the Baptist were expecting their Messiah to come. John as Jesus' forerunner recognized Him as the One sent by God at His baptism in water (John 1:32, 33). But just like many of the Jews at that time and including the disciples of Christ (Luke 19:11), John was expecting Jesus the Christ (*Messiah* in Hebrew) to reign as King of Israel in their lifetime (Acts 1:6,7; Luke 24:21). John the Baptist seemed to not see this thing happening while he was in prison. So he sent some of his disciples to Jesus to inquire if He was really the Messiah or should they expect another (Matthew 11:2,3). The Bible Knowledge Commentary puts it this way: "John must have thought, *If I am Messiah's forerunner and Jesus is the Messiah, why am I in prison?* John needed reassurance and clarification, for he had expected the Messiah to overcome wickedness, judge sin, and bring in His kingdom."[58] John's suffering in prison was something he could not reconcile with the supernatural confirmation by the Triune God of Jesus' Messiahship.

Jesus indeed was the Messiah to come. He first had to suffer and die on the cross (as prophesied in Isaiah 53: 3-5) so people will be saved from sin and have spiritual deliverance. But the Jews, including John the Baptist and the disciples of Christ, only understood and desired for the political deliverance (Isaiah 9:7) the Messiah would do which will happen during His Second Coming yet. McGee writes, "John's question

---

[58] John R. Walvoord (Editor) and Roy B. Zuck, *The Bible Knowledge Commentary-An Exposition of the Scriptures by Dallas Seminary Faculty-New Testament*, Notes on Matt. 11: 2-3.

is a logical one. He has every reason to believe that the King would have assumed power by this time. He is definitely puzzled that the Lord is moving so slowly toward the throne."[59]

---

[59] McGee, *Thru the Bible, 5 Volumes,* Notes on Matt. 11:3.

Alleged Contradiction # 44

44. According to the Gospel of John, what did Jesus say about bearing his own witness?
    (a) "If I bear witness to myself, my testimony is not true" (John 5: 31)
    (b) "Even if I do bear witness to myself, my testimony is true" (John 8:14)

Answer:

To get the context of what Jesus is saying in John 5:31, we need to read the verses before and after this, up to verse 37. So here they are:

John 5:30 "I can do nothing on My own initiative. As I hear, I judge; and My judgment is just, because I do not seek My own will, but the will of Him who sent Me.

John 5:31 "If I *alone* testify about Myself, My testimony is not true. NASB

Verse 31 should be interpreted along with the previous verse 30 or one gets a wrong interpretation (veers out of context). Verse 30 says that what Jesus hears from His Father, that is what He will say (judge) because He only wants to say the Father's will and not His own. So, when Jesus testifies, it is not really He Himself who testifies but the Father. If His testimony comes from Himself only and not from the Father, then that testimony would not be true. This is the interpretation of verse 31. The verses above is quoted from the NASB translation, which includes the word "alone" to get what Jesus intended to say in relation to the preceding verse. John 8:14 which says that Jesus' testimony is true is because He only seeks what the Father wants Him to speak. About this verse, The Cambridge Bible comments: "In John 8:14 we have an apparent contradiction to this, but it is only the other side of the same truth: 'My witness is true because it is really My Father's.'"[60]

---

[60] Ryle, *The Cambridge Bible for Schools and Colleges*, Notes on John 5:31.

Alleged Contradiction # 45

45. When Jesus entered Jerusalem did he cleanse the temple that same day?
    (a) Yes (Matthew 21:12)
    (b) No. He went into the temple and looked around, but since it was very late he did nothing. Instead, he went to Bethany to spend the night and returned the next morning to cleanse the temple (Mark 11:1-17)

Answer:

Christ made two trips to the temple … Mark 11:11 says that Christ entered the temple the day of His triumphal entry. When Christ enters the temple, Mark does not mention Christ making any proclamations against any wrongdoing. Verse 12 says, "Now the next day," referring to … the second day. Matthew, however, addresses the two trips of Christ to the temple as though they were one event. This gives the impression that the first day Christ entered the temple He drove out the buyers and sellers as well. Mark's account, however, gives more detail to the events, revealing that there were two trips to the temple. In view of this, we have no reason to believe that there is a discrepancy in the accounts.[61] Matthew's concern was only to write the events of Jesus' coming to the temple and cleansing it. He did not say, though, that these two events happened on the same day.

---

[61] Geisser and Howe, *The Big Book of Bible Difficulties*, p 354.

Alleged Contradiction # 46

46. The Gospels say that Jesus cursed a fig tree. Did the tree wither at once?
    (a) Yes. (Matthew 21:19)
    (b) No. It withered overnight (Mark 11:20)

Answer:

Matthew's narrative does not describe how many times Jesus went to the temple and what events happened at each time. The cursing of the fig tree and its withering was described as one event, not being specific that it happened in two days in all or the two times they passed by the tree. During the cursing of the fig tree the disciples, according to Mark, "heard" Jesus cursed the tree (Mark 11:14). They did not "see" it withered. The following day, as they passed by the fig tree, the disciples, according to Matthew, "saw" the fig tree withered (Matthew 21:20). The word used in Matthew 21:19 which is translated "immediately" or "at once" in many Bible translations can also be translated as "soon" according to Strong's Hebrew and Greek Dictionaries.[62] This does not necessarily mean "instantly."

---

[62] James Strong (author), *Strong's Exhaustive Concordance of the Bible with Greek and Hebrew Dictionaries.* (Peoria, IL: Royal Publishers, 1979). Entry on **G3916** (παραχρῆμα)

Alleged Contradiction # 47

47. Did Judas kiss Jesus?
    (a) Yes (Matthew 26:48-50)
    (b) No. Judas could not get close enough to Jesus to kiss him (John 18:3-12)

Answer:

Let us try to put together the story of the arrest of Jesus in the Garden of Gethsemane. All four gospel writers included this particular story in their records but did not put the same details. The three so-called synoptic gospels (Matthew, Mark and Luke) included in their records Judas' kissing Jesus (Matt. 26:49; Mark 14:45; Luke 22:47). The apostle John, however, writing much later, did not include that part of the story. He did not say, though, in his record that "Judas could not get close enough to Jesus to kiss him." This statement is somebody's guess. The fact is Judas was going before the crowd (Luke 22: 47; Mark 14: 43) so he would be the first one to reach Jesus (Mark 14:45). After kissing Jesus, he went to stand with the crowd (John 18:5). Jesus then asked them who they were looking for. They answered, "Jesus of Nazareth" (John 18:5). John 18:6 – "Now when He said to them, "I am *He*," they drew back and fell to the ground (NKJV). Judas standing with them could also have fallen to the ground. Jesus asked them again who they were looking for (John 18:7). After Jesus' second answer, they came forward to arrest Him (Matt. 26:50; Mark 14:46). These incidents, then, followed: Peter's cutting the ear of the high priest's servant (Matt. 26:51; Mark 14:47; Luke 22:50; John 18:10), Jesus commanding His disciples not to fight (Matt. 26:52; John 18:11), Jesus healing the servant's ear (Luke 22:51), Jesus' disciples fleeing (Matt. 26:56; Mark 14:50), Jesus bound (John 18:12) and Jesus was brought by the people to Annas, the ex-high priest (John 18:13).

John's record says that Judas was "standing with them" (John 18:5). But Luke's record says also that Judas "went before them... to kiss him" (Luke 22:47). Since kissing Jesus was the agreed sign for the soldiers to come forward and arrest the right person, Judas would naturally go back to stand with the crowd in order to give way for the soldiers to come forward and arrest Jesus. This means that Judas' going before the crowd and kissing Jesus happened first before he stood with the crowd and the soldiers' going forward to arrest Jesus. The omission by the writer John of what the three other gospel writers recorded would not mean that Judas did not kiss Jesus.

48. What did Jesus say about Peter's denial?
    (a) "The cock will not crow till you have denied me three times" (John 13:38).
    (b) "Before the cock crows twice you will deny me three times" (Mark 14:30). When the cock crowed once, the three denials were not yet complete (see Mark 14:72). Therefore prediction (a) failed.

Answer:

There are two possible ways of answering this Alleged Contradiction. The first one is from Geisser and Rowe's book: "It is possible that different accounts are due to an early copyist error in Mark, that resulted in the insertion of the "two" in early manuscripts (at Mark 14:30 and 72). This would explain why some important manuscripts of Mark mention only one crowing, just like Matthew and John, and why "two" appears at different places in some manuscripts.[63]

Gill's commentary on Mark 4:30 does not consider a copyist error. He says: "… for there was a first and second cock crowing, the one at midnight, and the other near break of day, and which last is properly the cock crowing…"[64] When I was growing up, lived In a more rural situation and the alarm clock were not yet as common in our place, we had the cock crowing as a way for people to wake up those who want to rise up before dawn. It happened around 4 a.m. One time I was awakened by a cock crowing. When I looked at my watch it was twelve midnight. I was surprised with that because I usually was awakened by the cock crowing at about 4 in the morning. I noticed that only a few

---

[63] Geisser and Howe, *The Big Book of Bible Difficulties*, p 360.

[64] Gill, *Exposition of the Entire Bible,* Notes on Matt. 14:30.

cocks would crow in midnight, not like the second cock crowing when one can hear so many, one after another.

Alleged Contradiction # 49

49. Did Jesus bear his own cross?
    (a) Yes (John 19:17)
    (b). No (Matthew 27:31-32)

Answer:

Clarke on Matthew 27: 32 says: "In John, Joh_19:16, Joh_19:17, we are told Christ himself bore the cross, and this, it is likely, he did for a part of the way; but, being exhausted with the scourging and other cruel usage which he had received, he was found incapable of bearing it alone; therefore they obliged Simon, not, I think, to bear it entirely, but to assist Christ, by bearing a part of it. It was a constant practice among the Romans, to oblige criminal to bear their cross to the place of execution."[65]

Because it was the practice at that time, Jesus had to carry His cross. Matthew's "going out" (27:32) is in present participle which means in Greek grammar a "continuous action or repeated action." This means Jesus with His cross and the soldiers were already on their way for some time. When Jesus was too exhausted physically to go further because of the many wounds inflicted on Him and was not able to carry it alone anymore, the soldiers compelled a certain Simon from Cyrene to carry Jesus' cross.

---

[65] Clarke, *Adam Clarke's Commentary on the Bible*, Notes on Matt. 27:32.

Alleged Contradiction # 50

50. Did Jesus die before the curtain of the temple was torn?
    (a) Yes (Matthew 27:50-51; Mark 15:37-38)
    (b) No. After the curtain was torn, then Jesus crying with a loud voice, said, "Father, into thy hands I commit my spirit!" And having said this he breathed his last (Luke 23:45-46)

Answer:

From *Baker's New Testament Commentary* we read this: "As often, so also now, Luke is not arranging his material chronologically when he mentions the tearing of this curtain before reporting the actual death of Christ. Matthew and Mark make clear that the rending of the veil followed immediately upon Christ's death; one might even say, "occurred at the moment of that death." *Through that death the way into the heavenly sanctuary was opened.*

"But something can be said also in favor of Luke's arrangement. It is again, as often, topical. He first mentions the material signs (the darkness and the rending of the veil), then the death, and then, without interruption, the effect of that death *upon people:* (a) upon the centurion, (b) upon the crowds, (c) upon the women from Galilee.[66]

To follow Luke's outline, it would be like this:

    A. The miraculous signs during Christ's death: (1) darkness at noon time which lasted for 3 hours and (2) the

---

[66] Hendriksen and Kistemaker, *New Testament Commentary Set*, 12 Volumes, Notes on Luke 23:45.

rending of the veil without any natural thing that caused it (Verses 44-45)

B. The account of the death of Christ (verse 46)

C. The results/effects of His death on the people around: (1) upon the centurion, (2) upon the people (crowds) and (3) upon His acquaintances including the women from Galilee (verses 47-49)

The first Greek word (*kai*) in verse 46 connecting the death of Christ to verse 45 (curtain torn in two) can be translated into many English conjunctions but primarily "and." Some Bible translations use the word "then" which is not in the original Greek. Even the King James and New King James translation of "and when" is adding a word which is not in the original. If Luke actually meant that Christ's death comes after the curtain was torn in two, he would have used another Greek word (*meta*, after) which he used abundantly throughout his gospel and the book of Acts.

Alleged Contradiction # 51

51. Did Jesus say anything secretly?
    (a) No. "I have said nothing secretly" (John 18:20)
    (b) Yes. "He did not speak to them without a parable, but privately to his own disciples he explained everything" (Mark 4:34). The disciples asked him "Why do you speak to them in parables?" He said "To you it has been given to know the secrets of the kingdom of heaven, but to them it has not been given" (Matthew 13: 10-11)

Answer:

Jesus preached in villages and taught in synagogues. Matt. 9:35 – "Then Jesus went about all the cities and villages, teaching in their synagogues, preaching the gospel of the kingdom, and healing every sickness and every disease among the people." So the people heard about Jesus's teachings. In the context of Matt. 13:10, 11, Jesus was talking about parables of the kingdom to people. Parables are to be interpreted. Even the disciples did not understand some of them. So He had to explain the meaning of the parables to them privately (Mark 4:10-13) and told them "To you it has been given to know the mystery of the kingdom of God; but to those who are outside, all things come in parables" (Matt. 13:11).

So there were teachings of Jesus for the world who did not follow Christ and there were teachings for the disciples which are called "the secrets or mysteries of the kingdom" (Matt. 13:11, Mar. 4:12.). These mysteries of the kingdom were not secret to His disciples but secret to the non-followers of Christ. Jesus did this to give "light to those who sincerely desire it."[67]

---

[67] MacDonald and Farstad, *Believer's Bible Commentary*, Notes on Mark 4:30-34

Alleged Contradiction # 52

52. Where was Jesus at the sixth hour on the day of the crucifixion?
    (a) On the cross (Mark 15: 23)
    (b) In Pilate's court (John 19:14)

Answer:

The author of *101 Contradictions in the Bible* must have meant Mark 15:33. In this verse we find Jesus on the cross at the "sixth hour." In John 19:14, at the "sixth hour" we find Pilate handing his decision for Jesus to be crucified. So the question is, Where was Jesus at the "sixth hour" on the day of His crucifixion?

First, let us note that the Jewish and the Roman reckoning of the time of the day are not the same. In the Roman time, the "sixth hour" is 6 a.m. as we reckon it now. The Jewish time reckoned the day beginning from our 6:00 a.m. onwards. So the "third hour" would be 9:00 a.m., when they began crucifying Jesus (Mark 15: 25).[68] The "sixth hour" then (Mark 15: 33) in the Jewish time would be 12:00 noon to us. Jesus was on the cross at that time. When John used the word "sixth hour" in John 19:14 with Jesus before Pilate, he used the Roman time which would be 6:00 a.m. The reason John used the Roman time was because he wrote his gospel much later in the first century (about 85 A.D.)[69] when much of the Jews were already scattered to different nations of the world which was under the Roman Empire that time due to the destruction of Jerusalem and the Jewish temple in 70 A.D. by the Roman forces. John, writing from the city of Ephesus in the Roman province of Asia, was writing primarily

---

[68] Robertson, *Word Pictures* in the New Testament (6 Vols), Notes on John 19:14

[69] Jack W. Hayford (General Editor), *Spirit Filled Life Bible (NKJV)*. (Nashville: Thomas Nelson Publishers, 1991). 1571

to the Greek and Roman readers and, so, would use the Roman time in order to be understood by them.[70]

---

[70] Robertson, *Word Pictures in the New Testament*, Notes on John 19:14

Alleged Contradiction # 53

53. The gospels say that two thieves were crucified along with Jesus. Did both thieves mock Jesus?
    (a) Yes (Mark 15:32)
    (b) No. One of them mocked Jesus, the other defended Jesus (Luke 23:43)

Answer:

On this Alleged Contradiction, I agree with MacArthur who in his Bible Commentary says "The two robbers joined in the reviling of Jesus, though one later repented (Luk_23:40-43)."[71]

Those who mocked Jesus while He was on the cross were those who passed by (Matt. 27:39, Mark 15: 29), the chief priests with the scribes and elders or rulers of Israel (Matt. 27:41, Mark 15:31, Luke 23: 35), the thieves (Matt. 27:44,) and the soldiers (Luke 23: 36, 37). John in his account of the crucifixion does not mention any of the groups mocking Jesus. Notice that only Luke wrote about the soldiers mocking Jesus. Only Luke also recorded of one of the thieves who repented (Luke 23:40 -42) which he placed after the soldiers mocked Jesus. The possible reason why Matthew and Mark did not mention about one of the thieves repenting later on, is because both Matthew and Mark did not record about the soldiers mocking Jesus which preceded one of the thieves' change of heart.

---

[71] MacArthur, *The MacArthur Bible Commentary*, Notes on Mark 15:32-34

Alleged Contradiction # 54

54. Did Jesus ascend to Paradise the same day of the crucifixion?
    (a) Yes. He said to the thief who defended him, "Today you will be with me in Paradise" (Luke 23:43)
    (b) No. He said to Mary Magdalene two days later, "I have not yet ascended to the Father" (John 20:17)

Answer:

This question comes from a person who does not understand the teaching of the Bible on paradise. Many believers do not have the biblical understanding on this, too. How much more to those who do not follow Christ. Before the ascension of Christ, this place called paradise is the same one that is called "Abraham's bosom" or, Abraham's side (Luke 16:22). This was located under the earth, but separated by an impassable "gulf" or chasm from the place of torment of those who do not follow God (Luke 16:26). After Christ's death and during His ascension, this place called "paradise" was transferred up to heaven. Ephesians 4:8-10 describes the transfer as "When He ascended to the heights, He led a crowd of captives" (verse 8, NLT) and brought them to a place that is higher than the heavens (verse 10). Later in the New Testament, Paul the Apostle had an experience of having gone to "paradise" (2 Cor. 12:4) which he also calls as "third heaven" (2 Cor. 12:2, the first heaven explained by many Bible scholars as the atmosphere where the birds fly (Gen. 1:20, 7:23, KJV, NKJV), the second is where there are heavenly bodies like stars, planets and constellations (Gen. 1:14-18, KJV, NKJV) and the third as the place where God's throne is (Matt. 5:34, 23:22; 2 Cor. 12:2, 12:4). So, during the death of Jesus Christ and the repentant thief, paradise was still under the earth to where both Jesus and thief went when Christ died (Eph. 4:9). After Christ's resurrection from the dead, He first showed Himself to Mary Magdalene before going up to heaven (John 20:17). Having gone to heaven, He then showed Himself to the other women (Matt. 28:9) who were hurrying from the tomb to tell the apostles of Christ's resurrection as told them by the angel they saw at Jesus' tomb (Matt. 28:5-7).

According to the Pulpit Commentary, paradise "in the ordinary language used by the Jews, of the unseen world ... signifies the 'Garden of Eden' or 'Abraham's bosom'..."[72] This could be one reason why Jesus used the word 'paradise' here - so that the repentant thief and the Jews around hearing Him would understand what He was saying about.

Another Bible commentary says that this place called paradise is "where the soul of Jesus was between His death and resurrection."[73]

---

[72] Spence and Exell, *The Pulpit Commentary,* Notes on Luke 23:43 under Luke 23: 1-56

[73] Schaff (Editor), *A Popular Commentary of the New Testament*, Notes on Luke 23:43

55. When Paul was on the road to Damascus he saw a light and heard a voice. Did those who were with him hear the voice?
    (a) Yes (Acts 9:7)
    (b) No (Acts 22:9)

Answer:

In Acts 9:7 Paul's companions heard "**a** voice" but saw no person speaking. In Acts 22:9 his companions did not hear "**the** voice of Him" (Jesus) who spoke to Paul. Note the definite article before the word "voice" in the latter use of the same word. The Greek word for "voice" used here according to James Strong can be translated "noise, sound or voice."[74] In Acts 9:7, it is better to translate the verse as saying that Paul's companions heard a noise or sound of a person speaking but did not see the person. Paul heard the voice of Jesus speaking to him but his companions heard only a sound or noise.

The word "hear" in the Greek also can be translated "be noised, be reported, understand."[75] It is best, therefore, to say that in Acts 9:7 Paul's companions heard a voice or sound but that in Acts 22: 9, they did not understand the voice they heard which was intended only for Paul. This is how it is translated in the NIV, NLT, NASB, ISV and other Bible

---

[74] James Strong (Author) *Strong Exhaustive Concordance of the Bible with Greek and Hebrew Dictionary*. (Nashville, TN: Crusade Bible Inc., 1990). Entry on Greek word G5456

[75] Ibid. Entry on Greek word G191

translations. A Bible commentary puts it this way: "so these men heard the *voice* that spake to Saul, but heard not the *articulate words.*"[76]

---

[76] Jamieson, Fausset and Brown, *Jamieson, Fausset, and Brown's Commentary on the Whole Bible,* Notes on Acts 9:7

56. When Paul saw the light he fell to the ground. Did his traveling companions also fall to the ground?
    (a) Yes (Acts 26:14)
    (b) No (Acts 9:7)

Answer:

The time of Paul and his companions falling to the ground and the time of God conversing with Paul did not happen at the same time, but the latter follows the former. Acts 9:7 does not expressly say that Paul's companions did not fall to the ground. If we put together the two accounts, we can say that when the heavenly light shone upon them (Acts 26:13), Paul and his companions fell to the ground (Acts 26:14). Paul's companions stood right after that while Paul, still on the ground, was having a conversation with God. While standing, Paul's companions heard the sound of God talking to Paul but did not understand the message intended only for Paul. That's why they stood speechless (Acts 9:7). About the end of God's conversation with Paul, He commanded him to rise (Acts 26:16)

Alexander MacLaren narrates the account thus: "The attendants had fallen to the ground like him, but seem to have struggled to their feet again, while he lay prostrate. They saw the brightness, but not the Person: they heard the voice, but not the words. Saul staggered by their help to his feet, and then found that with open eyes he was blind.[77]

Barnes has good notes on "stood speechless" of Acts 9:7. "**Stood speechless** - In Act_26:14, it is said that they all fell to the earth at the appearance of the light. But there is no contradiction. The narrative in

---

[77] Alexander MacLaren (Author), *Expositions of Holy Scriptures* (Classic Reprint). (London, UK: Forgotten Books, 2016). Notes on Acts 9:1-12

that place refers to the immediate effect of the appearance of the light. They were immediately smitten to the ground together. This was before the voice spake to Saul, Act 26:14. In this place Act 9:7 the historian is speaking of what occurred after the first alarm. There is no improbability that they rose from the ground immediately, and surveyed the scene with silent amazement and alarm. The word "speechless" ἐννεοὶ enneoi properly denotes "those who are so astonished or stupefied as to be unable to speak." In the Greek writers it means those who are deaf-mutes."[78]

---

[78] Barnes, *Barnes Notes on the Old and New Testaments,* Notes on Acts 9:7

Alleged Contradiction # 57

57. Did the voice spell out on the spot what Paul's duties were to be?
    (a) Yes (Acts 26:16-18)
    (b) No. The voice commanded Paul to go into the city of Damascus and there he will be told what he must do. (Acts 9:7; 22:10)

Answer:

Not mentioned in the Scripture references in this Alleged Contradiction above is Acts 9:15-16 where God told Ananias what His plans were for Paul. God also told Paul what His plans for him were in Acts 26: 16-18 when he had an encounter with Christ on the road to Damascus. Then in Acts 9:6 and Acts 22:10 God said to Paul to go to the city and he will be told what he shall do. What Ananias told Paul was to receive his healing from blindness and to be filled with God's Spirit (Acts 9:17). After this, Paul's submitting to baptism in water was another thing he did in Damascus. Sometime during Paul's stay and fellowship with the believers in Damascus (most probably after his water baptism), Ananias would tell Paul what God told him about His plans for Paul. This is in line with a very important teaching in Scriptures which is this: The follower of Christ who thinks he is hearing from God about His will or plan for his life should expect two or more confirmations from circumstances and from other Christian believers (specially from Christian leaders) about what God is telling him to do. (Examples of scriptures on this teaching: Deut. 19:15, Matt. 18:16, Acts 13:1-3, Acts 15:28, Acts 17:11.) So Paul in this case not only heard from God Himself but also from Ananias later on. Robertson describes this thus: "Paul blends the message of Jesus to Ananias with that [of Jesus Christ] to him as one."[79]

---

[79] Robertson, *Word Pictures in the New Testament,* Notes on Acts 9:15

Alleged Contradiction # 58

58. When the Israelites dwelt in Shittim they committed adul-
    tery with the daughters of Moab. God struck them with a
    plague. How many people died in that plague?
    (a) Twenty-four thousand (Numbers 25:1 and 9)
    (b) Twenty-three thousand (I Corinthians 10:8)

Answer:

The following answer is taken from *The Big Book of Bible Difficulties*:

"There are two possible explanations here. First, some have suggested
that the difference is due to the fact 1 Corinthians 10:8 is speaking only
about those who died "in one day" (23,000), whereas Numbers 25:9 is
referring to the complete number (24,000) that died in the plague.

"Others believe two different events are in view here. They note that
1 Corinthians 10:7 is a quote of Exodus 32:6 and indicates that the 1
Corinthians passage is actually referring to the judgment of God after the
idolatrous worship of the golden calf (Exodus 32). The Exodus passage
does not state the number of people that died as a result of the judgment of God, and the actual number is not revealed until 1 Corinthians
10:8. According to 1 Corinthians 10:8, 23,000 died as a result of the judgment of God for their worship of the golden calf. According to Numbers
25:9, 24,000 died as a result of the judgment of God for Israel's worship
of Baal at Baal-Peor."[80]

MacArthur has a further explanation on the second possible answer
related to the 23,000 in 1 Corinthians 10:8: "**twenty-three thousand**.
Having just quoted from Exodus 32 in verse 1Co 10:7, this very likely

---

[80] Geisser and Howe, *The Big Book of Bible Difficulties*, pp 109, 110

also refers to the incident in Exodus 32, not to the incident at Shittim in Numbers 25 ... Apparently, 3,000 were killed by the Levites (Exo_32:28) and 20,000 died in the plague (Exo_32:35)"[81]

---

[81] MacArthur, *The MacArthur Bible Commentary*, Notes on 1 Cor. 10:8

Alleged Contradiction # 59

59. How many members of the house of Jacob came to Egypt?
    (a) Seventy souls (Genesis 46:27)
    (b) Seventy-five souls (Acts 7:14)

Answer:

MacArthur notes that "Gen_46:26-27; Exo_1:5; Deu_10:22 give the figure as seventy. However, the LXX (the Greek translation of the OT, which Stephen as a Hellenist would have used) in Gen_46:27 reads "seventy-five.""[82] Different authors in modern times offer different suggestions why the Greek translation of the Old Testament has "seventy five" for Gen. 46:27. The religious scholars in Israel during that time being closer to the time of the translation of LXX would have a better reason why this is so.

From *Vincent's Word Studies,* we learn that "Hebrew was the [*sic rational*] *national* dialect, Latin the *official*, and Greek the *common* dialect."[83] MacLaren puts it this way: "'Hebrew,' the national tongue; 'Greek,' the common medium of intercourse between varying nationalities; and 'Latin' the official language."[84] Greek being the "common dialect" or the "common medium" of communication, Stephen would naturally use and quote from the common Scriptures used by the people so that he can be understood. This is the reason why he said "seventy five" in Acts 7:14 as this is the number written in the Greek translation of the Old Testament they were using at that time.

---

[82] Ibid. Notes on Acts 7:14

[83] Marvin R. Vincent (Author), *Word Studies in the New Testament (4 Volume Set).* (Grand Rapids, MI: Wm. B. Eerdmans Publishing Co, 1975). Notes on John 19:20

[84] MacLaren, *Expositions of Holy Scriptures,* Notes on John 19:20

Alleged Contradiction # 60

60. What did Judas do with the blood money he received for betraying Jesus?
    (a) He bought a field (Acts 1:18)
    (b) He threw all of it into the temple and went away. The priests could not put the blood money into the temple treasury, so they used it to buy a field to bury strangers (Matthew 27:5)

Answer:

From Thru the Bible with J. Vernon Mcgee:

"The apparent discrepancy in the two accounts as to the disposition of the money may be thus explained: "It was not lawful to take into the temple treasury, for the purchase of sacred things, money that had been unlawfully gained. In such case the Jewish law provided that the money was to be restored to the donor, and, if he insisted on giving it that he should be induced to spend it for something for the public weal. By a fiction of law the money was still considered to be Judas's, and to have been applied by him in the purchase of the well-known 'potter's field' (Edersheim, *Life of Jesus,* ii, 575)"[85]

Not all details can be recorded in any true story, the Bible not being an exception. The story could have been like this: Judas, sometime after agreeing with the chief priests for a sum of money (Matt. 26:14-16, Mark 14:10, 11), could have gone to the owner of the field and before finally deciding to buy it, tried to see the actual place himself. In going back to the owner to close the deal and pay for the field, Judas could have been

---

[85] McGee, *Thru the Bible, 5 Volumes;* Notes on Acts 1:15-18

overcome with guilt over his betrayal of Jesus, so he went to the priests instead of to the owner of the field.

There he acknowledged publicly his error and threw the money into the temple (Matt. 27:3-5). Then he went back to the field where there was a tree near the cliff, and hanged himself there (Matt. 27:5). The rope he used (probably his belt) broke or went loosed, so he fell on the sharp rocks below, gashing his stomach, causing his intestines to spill out (Acts 1:18). Since it was immoral for the priests to put blood money into the temple treasury (Matt. 27:6,7), the thirty pieces of silver suddenly became a big problem none of them wanted to touch. Probably learning that Judas had earlier intended to buy a field, knowing this either from Judas himself, or, later on, from the seller of the field who was waiting for the money, the priests decided to buy the field as burial place of strangers as a happy solution (Matt. 27:6-8).

Alleged Contradiction # 61

61. How did Judas die?
    (a) After he threw the money into the temple he went away
        and hanged himself (Matthew 27:5)
    (b) After he bought the field with the price of his evil deed
        he fell headlong and burst open in the middle and all
        his bowels gushed out (Acts 1:18)

Answer:

Here's the explanation from *The Big Book of Bible Difficulties*:

"These accounts are not contradictory, but mutually complementary. Judas hung himself exactly as Matthew affirms that he did. The account of Acts simply adds that Judas fell, and his body opened up at the middle and his intestines gushed out. This is the very thing one would expect of someone who hanged himself from a tree over a cliff and fell on sharp rocks below."[86]

---

[86] Geisser and Howe, *The Big Book of Bible Difficulties*, p 361

Alleged Contradiction # 62

62. Why is the field called "Field of Blood"?
    (a) Because the priests bought it with the blood money (Matthew 27:8)
    (b) Because of the bloody death of Judas therein (Acts 1:19)

Answer:

Both reasons for calling the burial place of foreigners as Field of Blood are correct. The chief priests who heard Judas' confession of him betraying an innocent blood (Matt. 27:3,4) called it the Field of Blood in their understanding of the situation (Matt. 27: 6-8). The people who only heard of Judas hanging himself in that field and burst open his intestines when falling on the cliff called it the Field of Blood in their own understanding of what happened (Acts 1:18,19). To the chief priests who heard Judas' confession, it was because of the innocent blood of the person he betrayed. To the people it was because of Judas hanging himself there and falling down the cliff spilling his intestines.

Alleged Contradiction # 63

63. Who is ransom for whom?
    (a) "The Son of Man came... to give his life as a ransom for many" (Mark 10:45). "Christ Jesus who gave himself as a ransom for all..." (1 Timothy 2: 5-6)
    (b) "The wicked is a ransom for the righteous, and the faithless for the upright" (Proverbs 21:18)

Answer:

There are many uses for the word "ransom" in the Bible. The following are examples (from NIV):

(Exo. 30:12) "When you take a census of the Israelites to count them, each one must pay the LORD a ransom for his life at the time he is counted. Then no plague will come on them when you number them." In this verse God promised the Israelis that no plague will come on them when they pay a certain amount (in shekel) at the time one is to be counted in the census. The shekel in this case was considered a ransom.

(Prov. 13:8) "A person's riches may ransom their life, but the poor cannot respond to threatening rebukes." There would be times in a person's life when he comes into a situation where deliverance is badly needed. At this time his riches may be able to help him out of the situation. In this case his riches is considered a ransom.

(Isa. 43:3) "For I am the LORD your God, the Holy One of Israel, your Savior; I give Egypt for your ransom, Cush and Seba in your stead." There was a time when Israel was under siege from their enemy. Through their prayers, the enemy turned to the bigger nation Egypt and other nations. This saved the nation of Israel. In this case Egypt and the other nations were considered as a ransom for Israel.

(Prov. 21:18) "The wicked become a ransom for the righteous, and the unfaithful for the upright."

Clarke explains this particular verse thus: "The wicked shall be a ransom for the righteous - God often in his judgments cuts off the wicked, in order to prevent them from destroying the righteous. And in general, we find that the wicked fall into the traps and pits they have digged for the righteous."[87]

In the use of the word 'ransom' here, the wicked people received God's judgments and, thereby, saving His people from those judgments or from their evil traps. In this case, the wicked people are considered a ransom.

All people have sinned (Rom. 3:23). They can never save themselves from their sins and from hell. Not even their good works or their righteous acts can save them which are considered "filthy rags" (Isa. 64:6). Only the sinless Christ can save them through His substitutionary death on the cross (Acts 4:12). Christ is the ransom for all people when they come to Him for mercy and forgiveness of their sins.

---

[87] Clarke, *Adam Clarke's Commentary on the Bible*, Notes on Prov. 21:18

Alleged Contradiction # 64

64. Is the Law of Moses useful?
    (a) Yes. "All scripture is... profitable..." (2 Timothy 3:16)
    (b) No. "... A former commandment is set aside because of its weakness and uselessness.." (Hebrews 7:18)

Answer:

To get the right interpretation of Heb. 7:18, let's take into consideration the verses before and after it:

Heb. 7:17 For it is declared: "You are a priest forever, in the order of Melchizedek."

Heb. 7:18 The former regulation is set aside because it was weak and useless

Heb. 7:19 (for the law made nothing perfect), and a better hope is introduced, by which we draw near to God. NIV

One rule for correct interpretation of Scriptures is to consider the context. Heb. 7:18 talks about something being "set aside because of its weakness and uselessness..." What is this being set aside? Both the verses before and after Heb. 7:18, as we can see above, talks about "a priest forever" (v. 17) "by which we draw near to God" (v. 19). This priest is no other than Jesus Christ (v. 24). This eternal priest replaces the Jewish priesthood which is now considered useless because Christ has already died on the cross for all and by Him we can now directly come to God and not anymore through the Jewish high priest. The Jewish high priest had to offer sacrifice not only for the people but also for himself since he also has sinned (Heb. 7:27). But this is not the case with the new high priest, Jesus Christ, the sinless One (v. 27). So, Heb. 7:18 is not talking about the Law of Moses to be set aside but the Jewish priest-hood. *The IVP Bible Background Commentary: New Testament* says: "Yet God had promised another priesthood, an eternal and hence change-less one (Heb_7:17; cf. Heb_7:3), which renders the first, imperfect one obsolete."[88]

---

[88] Craiz S. Keener (Author), *The IVP Bible Background Commentary: New Testament 02nd Edition.* (Downers Grove, IL: IVP Academic, 2014). Notes on Heb. 7:11-19

Alleged Contradiction # 65

65. What was the exact wording on the cross?
    (a) "This is Jesus the King of the Jews" (Matthew 27 :37)
    (b) "The King of the Jews" (Mark 15:26)
    (c) "This is the King of the Jews" (Luke 23:38)
    (d) "Jesus of Nazareth, the King of the Jews" (John 19:19)

Answer:

Let me summarize the answer to this Alleged Contradiction from *The Big Book of Bible Difficulties*. The phrase "the king of the Jews" is identical in all four Gospels. The difference is in what is omitted by them. It is possible that each Gospel only gives part of the complete statement. Below is the complete statement and what each Gospel writer has omitted in parenthesis.

Matthew: "This is Jesus [of Nazareth] the king of the Jews."

Mark: "[This is Jesus of Nazareth] the king of the Jews."

Luke: "This is [Jesus of Nazareth] the king of the Jews."

John: "[This is] Jesus of Nazareth the king of the Jews."

Thus, the whole statement may have read "This is Jesus of Nazareth, the king of the Jews." In this case, each Gospel is giving the essential part ('the king of the Jews"), but no Gospel writer is giving the complete inscription. But neither is any Gospel writer contradicting what the other Gospel writers say. The accounts are divergent and mutually complementary, not contradictory.[89]

---

[89] Geisser and Howe, *The Big Book of Bible Difficulties*, pp 361-362

Alleged Contradiction # 66

66. Did Herod want to kill John the Baptist?
    (a) Yes (Matthew 14:5)
    (b) No. It was Herodias, the wife of Herod who wanted to kill him. But Herod knew that He was a righteous man and kept him safe (Mark 6:20)

Answer:

Herod had John arrested and put in prison for speaking against his unlawful marriage to Herodias, his brother's wife (Matt. 14:3,4). While John was in prison, Herod had a great change of mind about John because of his awareness of the people's regard for John (Matt. 14:5) and because of his frequent visit to John in the prison to hear him (Mark 6:20) where he "liked to listen to him" (NIV), "heard him gladly" (NKJV), "used to enjoy listening to him" (NASB). He decided to "protect him" even though his wife wanted him killed (Mark 6:19,20). But when Herod's birthday came, he was so pleased with the dancing of Herodias' daughter that he promised her anything up to half of his kingdom (Mark 6:21-23). When at the suggestion of her mother she asked for John's head, Herod was "exceedingly sorry" (NKJV). But honoring what he had promised the young girl in front of his guests, he ordered the beheading of John (Mark 6:24-28).

So, back to the question. Did Herod want to kill John? At first, Yes, when he knew John spoke against his marriage with Herodias, wife of his brother. No, after he heard him in prison.

Alleged Contradiction # 67

67. Who was the tenth disciple of Jesus in the list of twelve?
    (a) Thaddaeus (Matthew 10: 1-4; Mark 3:13-19)
    (b) Judas son of James is the corresponding name in Luke's gospel (Luke 6:12-16)

Answer:

From the commentary authored by Keener we read: "Luk_6:13-16. People often had a secondary name, sometimes a nickname, which may account for the slight differences among the Gospels' lists of the Twelve, as well as for the distinguishing of two Simons, two Judases and the second James in the list (these names were common in this period)."[90]

Another commentary clarifies that Thaddaeus in Matthew is the same person as Judas son of James in Luke 6:12-16: "*Judas the son of James.* He is called Thaddaeus in Mat_10:3; Mar_3:18; and Lebbaeus in certain variants. He is in all probability "Judas not Iscariot" of Joh_14:22 (see on that passage); cf. Act_1:13."[91]

In the New Testament, people many times had more than one name. The *Wiersbe Bible Commentary NT* says: "The names of the Apostles are also given in Mat_10:1-4; Mar_3:16-19; Act_1:13 (minus Judas). In all the lists, Peter is named first and, except in Act_1:13, Judas is named last. The Judas in Act_1:13 is Judas the brother [more likely "the son"] of James, who is also called Thaddeus in Mar_3:18. It was not unusual for one man to have two or more names. Simon received the name *Peter*

---

[90] Keener, *The IVP Bible Background Commentary: New Testament 02nd Edition*, Notes on Luke 6:13-16

[91] Hendriksen and Kistemaker, *New Testament Commentary Set*, 12 Volumes, Notes on Luke 6:12-16

(stone) when Andrew brought him to Jesus (Joh_1:40-42). Bartholomew is the same as Nathanael (Joh_1:45-49). The other Simon in the group was nicknamed "Zelotes," which can mean one of two things."[92]

[92] Warren W. Wiersbe (Author), *Wiersbe Bible Commentary NT. (Wiersbe Bible Commentaries)* (Colorado, Springs: David C. Cook, 2007). Notes on Luke 6:12-16

Alleged Contradiction # 68

68. Jesus saw a man sit at the tax collector's office and called
    him to be his disciple. What was his name?
    (a) Matthew (Matthew 9:9)
    (b) Levi (Mark 2:14; Luke 5:27)

Answer:

The answer to Alleged Contradiction # 67 would answer this Alleged
Contradiction on the names of "Matthew" and "Levi." People then had
many names. On Mark 2:13, 14, the Pulpit Commentary has these notes:
There, not far from Capernaum, **he saw Levi, the son of Alphseus, sitting
at the receipt of custom** (ἐπὶ τὸ τελώνιον); more literally, *at the place
of toll.* This place would be in the direct line for traders from Damascus
to Accho, and a convenient spot for the receipt of the duties on the
shipping. It is observable that in St. Matthew's own Gospel (Mat 9:9)
he describes himself as "a man named Matthew." St. Luke, like St. Mark,
calls him Levi. The same person is no doubt meant. It is most likely that
his original name was Levi, and that upon his call to be an apostle he
received a new name, that of Matthew, or Mattathias, which, according
to Gesenius, means "the gift of Jehovah."[93]

---

[93] Spence and Exell, *The Pulpit Commentary,* Notes on Mark 2:13,14 under Mark
2:1-28

Alleged Contradiction # 69

69. Was Jesus crucified on the daytime before the Passover meal or the daytime after
    (a) After (Mark 14:12-17)
    (b) Before. Before the feast of the Passover (John 1) Judas went out at night (John 13:30). The other disciples thought he was going out to buy supplies to prepare for the Passover meal (John 13:29). When Jesus was arrested, the Jews did not enter Pilate's judgment hall because they wanted to stay clean to eat the Passover (John 18:28). When the judgment was pronounced against Jesus, it was about the sixth hour on the day of Preparation for the Passover (John 19:14)

Answer:

MacArthur comments on John 19:14 by explaining the two Passovers. "The chronological reckoning between John's Gospel and the synoptics [meaning, gospels of Matthew, Mark and Luke] does present a challenge in the accounts of the Last Supper (Joh_13:2). While the synoptics portray the disciples and the Lord at the Last Supper as eating the Passover meal on Thursday evening (Nisan 14) and Jesus being crucified on Friday, John's Gospel states that the Jews did not enter into the Praetorium "lest they should be defiled, but that they might eat the Passover" (Joh_18:28). So the disciples had eaten the Passover on Thursday evening, but the Jews had not. In fact, John (Joh_19:14) states that Jesus' trial and crucifixion were on the day of preparation for the Passover and not after the eating of the Passover. This means that since the trial and crucifixion occurred on Friday, Christ was actually sacrificed at the same time the Passover lambs were being slain (Joh_19:14). The question then becomes, "Why did the disciples eat the Passover meal on Thursday?"

"The answer lies in the fact that there were two distinct ways the Jews in Jesus' day reckoned the beginning and ending of days. Jews in northern Palestine calculated days from sunrise to sunrise. At least one non regional group, the Pharisees, used that system of time-keeping. But the Jews in southern Israel, which centered in Jerusalem, calculated the day from sunset to sunset. In contrast to the Pharisees, the priests and Sadducees, who for the most part lived around Jerusalem, followed the southern scheme.

"In spite of the confusion these two calendars must have created at times, they were kept for practical reasons. During the Passover season, for instance, it allowed for the feast to be celebrated legitimately on two adjoining days. This also permitted the temple sacrifices to be made over a total of four hours rather than two. The size of the population made this a complicated project. By lengthening the time for sacrifices, the double calendar had the effect of reducing both regional religious clashes between the differing groups.

"The double calendar easily explains the apparent contradiction in the Gospel accounts. Being Galileans (northerners), Jesus and the disciples considered Passover day to have started at sunrise on Thursday and end at sunrise on Friday. The Jewish leaders who arrested and tried Jesus, being mostly priests and Sadducees, considered Passover day to begin at sunset on Thursday and end at sunset on Friday. This explains how Jesus could thereby legitimately celebrate the last Passover meal with His disciples and yet still be sacrificed on Passover day.

"In these meticulous details one can see how God sovereignly and marvelously provided for the precise fulfillment of His redemptive plan. Jesus was anything but a victim of men's wicked schemes, much less of blind circumstance. Every word He spoke and every action He took were divinely directed and secured. Even the words and actions by others against Him were divinely controlled (Joh_11:49-52; Joh_19:11)."[94]

---

[94] MacArthur, *The MacArthur Bible Commentary*, Notes on John 19:14

Alleged Contradiction # 70

70. Did Jesus pray to the Father to prevent the crucifixion?
    (a) Yes. (Matthew 26:39); Mark 14:36; Luke 22:42)
    (b) No. (John 12:27)

Answer:

The answer "yes" in letter (a)   above is not accurate. The three verses of Scriptures cited in letter (a)   do not say that Jesus prayed to the Father to prevent the crucifixion. Matthew 26:39, for example, says: "O My Father, if it is possible, let this cup pass from Me; nevertheless, not as I will, but as You *will*." If this prayer of Christ was "O My Father, let this cup pass from Me," and no qualifying condition of "if it is possible," then the answer to the question is "yes." Jesus always wanted the Father's will to be done. The whole sentence in this verse includes "nevertheless, not as I will, but as You will."

The fact of Jesus' being one person in two natures (divine and human) is something that many people, even Christians, do not perfectly understand. For one thing, this applies only to Christ. Christ did not use the prerogatives of His deity while on earth (Phil. 2:5- 8) but depended solely on the power of the Holy Spirit to fulfill His calling on earth (Luke 4: 18,19; Acts 10:28; Acts 10:38; Acts 1:2, etc.). Christ set aside the prerogatives of His divinity and did not use them. In His humanity, Christ's human nature, though sinless, desires protection and pleasures for the human body. It was just like Adam and Eve before they sinned. The only thing with Jesus was, He wanted to completely obey the Father, so that whatever desires He had while in His human body that did not conform to the Father's will - He did not want to do them, though He felt them in His human form. So, on the eve of His crucifixion, He fully realized and was fully aware of what His human body will go through the following day - all the indescribable torture, humiliation and horrendous pain He would have to go through at the hands of the Roman soldiers. Christ's human nature cried out to God cringing from all of these. Aside from the physical pain, there would be the accusations and the condemnations which were not true that would come from the authorities and the people. So, Christ's human nature while in His physical body would naturally cry out to God to be spared from all of these. And yet, knowing that dying on the cross was the purpose for His coming to earth, His will was determined to say, "Nevertheless, not as I will, but Your will be done." In answer to this prayer, the Father sent an angel to strengthen Him (Luke 22:43). Because of this, Christ's intention to obey the Father as shown in John 12:27 was realized. Temptations or trials aimed at our humanity are not sin. Yielding to them are. A person has a will (ability to choose), emotion (ability to feel) and intelligence (ability to know and to be aware). Jesus as a person in His humanity had the ability to feel and, being aware of the extreme sufferings He had to go through the following day, asked to be spared of this. But Jesus as a person with a will (the ability to choose), decided to say "Nevertheless, not as I will, but Your will be done."

Alleged Contradiction # 71

71. In the gospels which say that Jesus prayed to avoid the cross, how many times did he move away from his disciples to pray?
    (a) Three (Matthew 26: 36-46 and Mark 14:32-42)
    (b) One. No opening is left for another two times. (Luke22:39-46)

Answer:

The answer "three" above is indeed supported in the Scriptures in Matthew 26:44 and Mark 14:41. The answer "one" is not; it's only an interpretation of the reading in Luke 22:39-46. Luke does not say in this particular passage that Christ moved away from his disciples to pray "one" time.

Luke included in his account the appearance of an angel to strengthen Him which all the other gospel writers did not include. In the three times that Christ moved away from Peter, James and John, He prayed the "same words" (Matthew 26:44, Mark 14:39). What Luke recorded must be the last time He prayed because after that prayer the angel appeared to strengthen Him, and, after rising up from prayer and coming back to His disciples, the crowd led by Judas Iscariot came while He was still speaking (Luke 22:42-47).

Alleged Contradiction # 72

72. Matthew and Mark agree that Jesus went away and prayed three times. What were the word of the second prayer?
    (a) Mark does not give the words but he says that the words were the same as the first prayer (Mark 14:39)
    (b) Matthew gives us the words, and we can see that they are not the same as in the first (Matthew 26:42)

Answer:

Gill gives this commentary on Mark 14:39: "**and prayed and spake the same words**; or word, that is, the same matter; for λογος [logos], here, ... which signifies a thing, or matter, as well as word: Christ prayed to the same effect, for matter and substance the same as before, though not in the same express words, as is clear from Mat_26:39."[95]

May I add to the commentary above by saying that "same words" in Matthew 26:44 also uses the same Greek word "logos" as in Mark 14:39. The first meaning of this word in Vine's dictionary is "(a) as embodying a conception or idea, e.g., Luk_7:7; 1Co_14:9, 1Co_14:19; "[96] The records in Matthew of the three times Jesus prayed in the garden of Gethsemane may not have the same exact words but they embody the same concept or idea. More explanation on this in the next Alleged Contradiction.

---

[95] Gill, *Exposition of the Entire Bible,* Notes on Mark 14:39

[96] W.E. Vine (Author), *Vine's Complete Expository Dictionary of Old and New Testament Words.* (Nashville, Tennessee: Thomas Nelson publisher, 1996). Notes on "Word," 1. *logos*

Alleged Contradiction # 73

73. What did the centurion say when Jesus died?
    (a) "Certainly this man was innocent" (Luke 23:47)
    (b) "Truly this man was the Son of God" (Mark 15: 39)

Answer:

From *The Big Book of Bible Difficulties* we read: "He may have said both. The centurion's words need not be limited to one phrase or sentence. The centurion could have said both things. In accordance with his own emphasis on Christ as the perfect man, Luke may have chosen to use this phrase rather than the ones used by Matthew and Mark. There is no major difference between Matthew and Mark, for in Greek the word "man" is implied by the masculine singular use of the word "this." It is also possible that Luke may have been paraphrasing or drawing an implication from what was actually said.

"Christian scholars do not claim to have the exact words of the speakers in every case, but only an accurate rendering of what they really said. First of all, it is generally agreed that they spoke in Aramaic, but the Gospels were written in Greek. So the words we have in the Greek text on which the English is based are already a translation. Second, the Gospel writers, like writers today, sometimes summarized or paraphrased what was said. In this way, it is understandable that the renderings will be slightly different. But in this case, as in all other cases, the essence of what was originally said is faithfully produced in the original text. While we do not have the exact words, we do have the same meanings. Finally, when the sentences are totally different (but not contradictory), then we may reasonably assume that both things were said on that occasion and that one writer uses one and another writer the other. This is a common literary practice even today."[97]

Here is an additional explanation that relates to Alleged Contradiction # 72 and # 73. Direct quote or "word for word" (verbatim) quotation is unknown in ancient cultures where writing and reading are not as common compared to today. In our modern world there is so much paper to write and books to read due to the invention of paper and the printing press. We've developed some new rules in the written language which the ancient cultures did not have. The Koine Greek that was used to write the New Testament does not have a sign for quote and unquote (" ") which indicates the exact words of what a person is saying. So, saying the intent, the concept or summary of what a person had said was very common. Every time you see the sign of quote and unquote in the English Bible, you see something supplied by the modern translators in order to make it understandable or easier to read by the modern readers.

---

[97] Geisser and Howe, *The Big Book of Bible Difficulties*, pp 364-365

Alleged Contradiction # 74

74. When Jesus said "My God, my God, why has thou forsaken Me?" in what language did he speak?
    (a) Hebrew: the words are "Eloi, Eloi…" (Matthew 27:46) [sic: should be "Eli, Eli"]
    (b) Aramaic: the words are "Eloi, Eloi…" (Mark 15:34)

Answer:

Ryle's comment on Matthew 27:46: "*Eli, Eli, lama sabachthani?*] (*Psa_22:1*). *Eli* is the Hebrew form. In <u>Mar_15:34</u> the Aramaic words are preserved exactly as they were pronounced by Jesus."[98]

A common dialect in Israel during the time of Jesus was Aramaic, a language they learned to speak when the nation was in captivity and away from their country, first during the Assyrian and then the Babylonian Empire. The Jews' Scriptures was in Hebrew which was read and expounded in the synagogues throughout the nation. Since Greek was the international language used by the Roman Empire which ruled the nations then including Israel, this language was also spoken in Israel. In fact, the New Testament books were written in Greek. Jesus, then, was a tri-lingual, at least.[99]

Though Jesus spoke Matthew 27:46 in Aramaic as preserved by Mark, Matthew used the Hebrew form of "My God, My God," left the rest of the sentence in Aramaic, and then gave a Greek translation. Since Matthew was writing mainly to the Hebrew people not only in Israel

---

[98] Ryle, The Cambridge Bible for Schools and Colleges, Notes on Matthew 27:46

[99] Jack Wellman, "What Language Did Jesus Speak? Was it Aramaic or Hebrew?" http://www.patheos.com/blogs/christiancrier/2014/10/04/what-language-did-jesus-speak-was-it-aramaic-or-hebrew/ (accessed March 14, 2017)

but those living in other nations, and since his gospel account keeps on referring to the Hebrew Scriptures, this use of the Hebrew form for "My God" would certainly connect to his audience.

Alleged Contradiction # 75

75. According to the gospels, what were the last words of Jesus before he died?
    (a) "Father, into thy hands I commit my spirit!" (Luke 23:46)
    (b) "It is finished" (John 19:30)

Answer:

It would be good to write out fully the two references above and not just quote a portion of them in order to understand them better. So here they are: (Note that both references talk about Jesus' spirit.)

(Luk 23:46) And Jesus, crying out with a loud voice, said, "Father, INTO YOUR HANDS I COMMIT MY SPIRIT." Having said this, He breathed His last. NASB

(Joh 19:30) Therefore when Jesus had received the sour wine, He said, "It is finished!" And He bowed His head and gave up His spirit. NASB

A commentary published by Baker's Publishing Group under its notes on John 19: 26-27 includes a list of the seven words or sayings of Jesus on the cross. Here they are with their references:[100]

1. "Father, forgive them: for they do not know what they are doing" (Luk_23:34)

2. "Today you will be with me in Paradise" (Luk_23:43)

---

[100]Hendriksen and Kistemaker, *New Testament Commentary Set*, 12 Volumes, Notes on John 19:26-27 under entry on John 19:17-37

3. "Woman, look! Your son! ... Look! Your mother!" (Joh_19:26-27)

4. "My God, my God, why hast thou forsaken me?" (Mat_27:46; Mar_15:34)

5. "I am thirsty" (Joh_19:28)

6. "It is finished" (Joh_19:30)

7. "Father, into thy hands I commend my spirit" (Luk_23:46).

Of the seven sayings on the cross, John records three, Luke records three, Matthew and Mark records only one. What John recorded (three sayings) is not recorded by any of the other gospels writers. The same is true with what Luke recorded (three sayings). What Matthew and Mark recorded (one saying) is not recorded in any of the other writers. None of the writers claims that what he recorded is/are the only saying(s) Jesus uttered on the cross. If one writer recorded all that Jesus said and done in His entire ministry then there would be no need for any other writer to write anything. That's impossible because the gospel writers wrote to different audiences with different specific situations and circumstances and, therefore, would choose words and deeds of Jesus that would fit their respective audiences well. Each writer would have a specific purpose of writing based on his type of audience and would necessarily include by the help of the Holy Spirit those information that would fit his audience. To get the whole story, therefore, of what Jesus said and did would be to compare all the gospel stories and try to put together what might chronologically and logically have happened in Jesus life.

In the case of the saying of Jesus recorded by Luke ("Father into thy hands I **commit my spirit**"), it is best to connect this saying with John's "And he bowed his head and **gave up His spirit**." Luke and John are both talking about Jesus' spirit here. According to John bowing His head and giving up His spirit happened **after** Jesus said, "It is finished." So, this (last or seventh) saying according to Luke fits well with John's saying "**And** He bowed His head and **gave up His spirit**" which statement comes after Jesus' saying, "It is finished." For sure, neither John nor Luke is saying in their writings that "this saying" is the last saying.

So it is up for us to figure out which one would be the last one. The one recorded by Luke, then ("I commend my spirit"), would follow John's recorded "It is finished."

Alleged Contradiction # 76

76. When Jesus entered Capernaum he healed the slave of a centurion. Did the centurion come personally to request Jesus for this?
    (a) Yes (Matthew 8:5)
    (b) No. He sent some elders of the Jews and his friends (Luke 7:3,6)

Answer:

From Geisser and Howe, we have this Answer:

"Both Matthew and Luke are correct. In the 1st century, it was understood that when a representative was sent to speak for his master, it was as if the master was speaking himself. Even in our day this is still the case. When the Secretary of State meets individuals from other countries he goes out in the name of the president of the United States. In other words, what he says, the president says. Therefore, Matthew states that a centurion came entreating Jesus about his sick slave, when in fact the centurion sent others on his behalf. So, when Matthew declares that the centurion was speaking, this was true, even though he was (as Luke indicated) speaking through his official representative."[101]

---

[101]Geisser and Howe, *The Big Book of Bible Difficulties*, p 334

77. (a) Adam was told that if and when he eats the forbidden fruit he would die the same day (Genesis 2:17)
    (b) Adam ate the fruit and went on to live to a ripe old age of 930 years (Genesis 5:5)

Answer:

From Geisser and Howe again, here's the Answer:

"The word "day" (*yom*) does not always mean a 24-hour day. For "one day" (*yom*) is as a thousand years" (Ps. 90:4; cf. 2 Pet. 3:8). Adam did die within a "day" in this sense... "he also died spiritually the exact instant he sinned (Eph. 2:1)." Anyone of these two senses of meaning would fulfill the pronouncement of God in Gen. 2:17."[102]

---

[102]Ibid. p 34

78. (a) God decided that the life span of humans will be limited to 120 years (Genesis 6:3)
    (b) Many people born after that lived longer than 120. Arpachshad lived 438 years. His son Shelah lived 433 years. His son Eber lived 464, etc. (Genesis 11:12-16)

Answer:

Here is an explanation from Keil and Delitzch on the 120 years:

"Therefore his days shall be 120 years:" this means, not that human life should in future never attain a greater age than 120 years, but that a respite of 120 years should still be granted to the human race. This sentence, as we may gather from the context, was made known to Noah in his 480th year, to be published by him as "preacher of righteousness" (2Pe 2:5) to the degenerate race."[103] After the lapse of 120 years, God called Noah and his household to enter the ark with the animals (Gen. 7:1-5). The following verse says that Noah was 600 years old when the floodwaters came in.

MacArthur says the same thing. He says that what God said about the 120 years is "the span of time until the flood (cf. 1Pe 3:20), in which man was given opportunity to respond to the warning that God's Spirit would not always be patient."[104]

---

[103]Keil and Delitzch, *Keil & Delitzsch Commentary of the Old Testament*, Notes on Gen. 6:3

[104]MacArthur, *The MacArthur Bible Commentary*, Notes on Gen. 6:3

Alleged Contradiction # 79

79. Apart from Jesus did anyone else ascend to heaven?
    (a) No (John 3:13)
    (b) Yes. "And Elijah went up by a whirlwind into heaven" (2 Kings 2:11)

Answer:

The Bible talks of three heavens. The first one is what we normally call the sky where the birds or the airplanes fly. Look at these verses:

(Job 35:11) Who teaches us more than the beasts of the earth, And makes us wiser than the <u>birds of heaven</u>?'

Also see verses like Jer. 7:33; Dan. 2:38; Rev. 19:7)

The second place also referred to as heaven in the Bible are where the stars and heavenly bodies are. Read the following:

(Isa. 13:10) For the <u>stars of heaven</u> and their constellations Will not give their light; The sun will be darkened in its going forth, And the moon will not cause its light to shine.

Also: Gen. 22:17, Deut. 1:10, Nahum 3:16, Matt. 24:29 and many more.

The Apostle Paul talks of the third heaven. This is the place where God's people will go when they die and leave their bodies on earth (2 Cor. 5:6, 8 - to be absent from the body is to be present with the Lord). Here's the verse Paul said about the third heaven:

(2Cor. 12:2) I know a man in Christ who fourteen years ago—whether in the body I do not know, or whether out of the body I do not know, God knows—such a one was caught up to the <u>third heaven</u>.

Elijah went up only to the first heaven and then out of Elisha's sight. Just like Moses, God must have buried Elijah somewhere where God, in His wise counsel, only knows.

Deut. 34:5 So Moses the servant of the LORD died there in the land of Moab, according to the word of the LORD.

Deut. 34:6 And He <u>buried him</u> in a valley in the land of Moab, opposite Beth Peor; but no one knows his grave to this day.

Michael the archangel must have known where Moses' body was buried (Jude 1:9).

In answer to the question above, Elijah went only to the first heaven and, like Moses, must have been buried by God Himself somewhere. John 3:13 says that only Jesus has ascended to heaven, third heaven, that is. Paul in his spirit went to the third heaven. This is not called ascension. Jesus' ascension was seen by the apostles and many other disciples (Acts 1:9-15) because His Spirit went up with a glorified or resurrected body (unlike Paul) having just been resurrected from the grave.

Alleged Contradiction # 80

80. Who was high priest when David went into the house of God and ate the consecrated bread?
    (a) Abiathar (Mark 2:26)
    (b) Ahimelech, the father of Abiathar (I Samuel 1:1; 22:20)

Answer:

Let's get the answer to this Alleged Contradiction from MacArthur:

"in the days of Abiathar the high priest. The phrase "in the days" can mean "during the lifetime." According to 1Sa_21:1, Ahimelech was the priest who gave the bread to David. Abiathar was Ahimelech's son, who later was the high priest during David's reign. Since Ahimelech died shortly after this incident (cf. 1Sa_22:19-20), it is likely that Mark simply added this designation to identify the well-known companion of David who later became the high priest, along with Zadok (2Sa_15:35).

Abiathar was the next high priest succeeding his father Ahimelech who died shortly after at the hands of King Saul most probably because this high priest showed kindness to David whom King Saul was pursuing to kill. There is a thought that seems lacking to the modern mind but presumed by Mark as obvious in his account in Mark 2:26. Bible translators supplied this lack with "in the days" (NKJV, NIV) of Abiathar the high priest or "during the lifetime" (ISV) of Abiathar the high priest. The Greek text in Mark 2:26 does not say Abiathar *was* the high priest *when* David ate the bread. It only indicates that the word "high priest" was a title given to Abiathar who did succeed his father. So the correct interpretation of Mark 2:26 is that David ate of the bread when Ahimelech was (still) the high priest. This happened "during the life time of" or "in the days of " Abiathar who became high priest shortly thereafter, the latter's official title also being, Abiathar the high priest."[105]

---

[105]Ibid. Notes on Mark 2:26

Alleged Contradiction # 81

81. Was Jesus' body wrapped in spices before burial in accordance with Jewish burial customs?
    (a) Yes and his female disciples witnessed his burial (John 19:39-40)
    (b) No. Jesus was simply wrapped in a linen shroud. Then the women bought and prepared spices "so that they may go and anoint him [Jesus]" (Mark 16:1)

Answer:

Let's get the answer to this Alleged Contradiction from two sources. First, from *The Pulpit Commentary*'s exposition on Mark 16:1:

"And when the sabbath was past, Mary Magdalene, and Mary the mother of James, and Salome, bought spices (ἠγόρασαν ἀρώματα) that they might come and anoint him. A hasty but lavish embalming of our Lord's sacred body had been begun on Friday evening by Joseph and Nicodemus. They had "brought a mixture of myrrh and aloes, about a hundred pound weight" (Joh_19:39). This would be a compound—the gum of the myrrh tree, and a powder of the fragrant aloe wood mixed together, with which they would completely cover the body, which was then swathed with linen cloths (ὀθόνια), also steeped in the aromatic preparation. Then the sindon would be placed over all. Compare the ἐνετύλιξεν, of St. Luke (Luk_23:53), as applying to the *sindon*, with the ἔδησαν of St. John (Joh_21:1-25:40) as applying to the ὀθόνια. This verse records a further stage in the embalming. What had been done on the Friday evening had been done in haste, and yet sufficiently for the preservation of the sacred body, if that had been needful, from decay. The remaining work could be done more carefully and tenderly at the tomb. Observe the aorist in this verse [ēgorasan] "they bought;" not "they had bought.""[106]

Here is an addition from *Word Pictures in the New Testament* on this same verse:

"**Bought spices** (*ēgorasan arōmata*). As Nicodemus did on the day of the burial (Joh_19:40)... They could buy them after sundown. Salome in the group again as in Mar_15:40. See Mat_28:1 for discussion of "late on the sabbath day" and the visit of the women to the tomb before sundown. They had returned from the tomb after the watching late Friday afternoon and had prepared spices (Luk_23:56). Now they secured a fresh supply."[107] While Mark 16:1 tells of women bringing spices to anoint Jesus' body, this verse does not say that the reason the women did this was because no spices had been applied and that "Jesus was simply wrapped in a linen shroud." The women brought a fresh supply of spices because what was done on Friday (John 19:39-40) was not sufficient.

---

[106]Spence and Exell, *The Pulpit Commentary,* Notes on Mark 16:1

[107]Robertson, *Word Pictures in the New Testament,* Notes on Mark 16:1

Alleged Contradiction # 82

82. When did the women buy the spices?
    (a) After "the Sabbath was past" (Mark 16:1)
    (b) Before the Sabbath. The women "prepared spices
        and ointments." Then, "on the Sabbath they rested
        according to the commandment." (Luke 23:55 to 24:1)

Answer:

Gill says this: "**had bought sweet spices**; ... for though the women might
have bought some on the preparation day, the day before the sabbath,
the same evening that Christ was buried, Luk 23:56, yet, they might buy
more for the same purpose, after the sabbath was over: for this there
was a particular market at Jerusalem (d); for we are a told, that "there
were there three markets, one by another; in the first of which were
sold, all kinds of precious things, silks, and embroidered work; in the
second, various kinds of fruits and herbs; and in the third, all kinds of
spices."[108] Gill is saying here that the women bought spices before and
after the Sabbath.

---

[108]Gill, *Exposition of the Entire Bible,* Notes on Mark 16:1

Alleged Contradiction # 83

83. At what time of day did the women visit the tomb?
    (a) "Toward the dawn" (Matthew 28:1)
    (b) "When the sun had risen" (Mark 16:2)

Answer:

The writer of this article (*101 Contradictions in the Bible*) does not state the version of Matthew 28:1 the verse above is taken from. Since Mark 16:2 above uses the New King James Version, let's use this same version for Matthew 28:1. It says, "Now after the Sabbath, as the first *day* of the week began to dawn, Mary Magdalene and the other Mary came to see the tomb." Note that it says, "began to dawn" and not "toward the dawn" as stated in the Alleged Contradiction above.

Mark 16: 1,2 in NKJV says: "Mar 16:1 Now when the Sabbath was past, Mary Magdalene, Mary *the mother* of James, and Salome bought spices, that they might come and anoint Him.

Mar 16:2 Very early in the morning, on the first *day* of the week, they came to the tomb when the sun had risen.

Comparing the verses above, we see that Matthew's "began to dawn," is connected to the women's "to see the tomb." So here, the women had not yet arrived to the tomb. Mark's "when the sun had risen" is connected to "came to the tomb." Here, the women already "came to the tomb." There is, therefore, no contradiction here on the time of the women's visit to the tomb. In Matthew's "began to dawn," the women had not yet arrived at the tomb.

Alleged Contradiction # 84

84. What was the purpose for which the women went to the tomb?
    (a) To anoint Jesus' body with spices (Mark 16:1; Luke 23:55 to 24:1)
    (b) To see the tomb. Nothing about the spices here (Matthew 28:1)
    (c) For no specified reason. In this gospel the wrapping with spices had been done before the Sabbath (John 20:1)

Answer:

Matthew's not mentioning about the spices the women brought with them does not mean they did not bring spices with them. If Matthew here said "Mary Magdalene and the other Mary came to see the tomb *without bringing spices*," then Matthew would have contradicted with Mark and Luke. But that is not the case. When a record is silent on one thing, it is wrong to conclude that that one thing is not there or did not happen. The "(c) ...Wrapping with spices had been done before the Sabbath (John 20:1)" could not be found in the verse reference cited. Maybe the writer of this "*101 Contradictions in the Bible*" is referring to what is found in John 19: 39-40 (in the NIV), the verses before John 20:1, which says:

Joh 19:39 He was accompanied by Nicodemus, the man who earlier had visited Jesus at night. Nicodemus brought a mixture of myrrh and aloes, about seventy-five pounds.

Joh 19:40 Taking Jesus' body, the two of them wrapped it, with the spices, in strips of linen. This was in accordance with Jewish burial customs.

On the wrapping of Jesus' dead body with spices as having been done previously before the women came on that resurrection morning, here is a commentary from Hendriksen and Kistemaker:

"It is true that Joseph of Arimathea and Nicodemus had already wound linen bandages around the body, strewing in a mixture of myrrh and aloes. But the dead body had not as yet been anointed. The living body [of Jesus] had been anointed (Mar 14:3-9) but not the dead one. Besides, a week had gone by since that other anointing had taken place.[109] Note that in Mark 16:1 the women's purpose for coming was "to anoint Jesus' body.""

Here's an additional explanation from Keener:

"Mar 16:1. Bodies were normally anointed with oil (then rinsed with water) before burial, but because Jesus had died on Friday just before the sabbath began (at sundown, around 6 P.M.), this anointing had been postponed. Men were allowed to dress only men for burial, but women could dress men or women."[110]

By the way, in John 20:1 only Mary Magdalene, not the women, were in the tomb of Jesus.

---

[109]Hendriksen and Kistemaker, *New Testament Commentary Set*, 12 Volumes, Notes on Mark 16:1

[110]Keener, *The IVP Bible Background Commentary: New Testament 02nd Edition*, Notes on Mark 16:1

85. A large stone was placed at the entrance of the tomb. Where was the stone when the women arrived?

(a) They saw that the stone was "Rolled back" (Mark 16:4). They found the stone "rolled away from the tomb" (Luke 24:2). They saw that "the stone had been taken away from the tomb" (John 20:1)

(b) As the women approached, an angel descended from heaven, rolled away the stone, and conversed with the women. Matthew made the women witness the spectacular rolling away of the stone (Matthew 28:1-6)

Answer:

Let us examine Matthew 28:1-6 below:

Mat 28:1 Now after the Sabbath, as the first *day* of the week began to dawn, Mary Magdalene and the other Mary came to see the tomb.

Mat 28:2 And behold, there was a great earthquake; for an angel of the Lord descended from heaven, and came and rolled back the stone from the door, and sat on it.

Mat 28:3 His countenance was like lightning, and his clothing as white as snow.

Mat 28:4 And the guards shook for fear of him, and became like dead *men.*

Mat 28:5 But the angel answered and said to the women, "Do not be afraid, for I know that you seek Jesus who was crucified.

Mat 28:6 He is not here; for He is risen, as He said. Come, see the place where the Lord lay. NKJV

Verse 1 above says "Mary Magdalene and the other Mary came to see the tomb." "To see the tomb" in verse 1 tells us that the women have not yet arrived the tomb. In verse 2, there was "a great earthquake; for an angel of the Lord descended from heaven, and came and rolled back the stone from the door and sat on it." This verse does not say about the women seeing this happening. The words "as the women approached" according to the writer of "*101 Contradictions in the Bible*" is his own interpretation and cannot be read in the Bible. It does not say in this passage in Matthew that the women saw the guards. The experience of the women in verse 5 tells us of the angel encouraging them. This, of course, happened when they already arrived at the tomb for the angel said, "Come and see the place where the Lord lay." Though the NKJV translates the first word of verse 5 as "But," the Greek word here is actually the same as in verse 4 which is translated "And." This observation is important because the word "but" tends to connect verse 5 with verse 4 where the guards shook for fear of the angel sitting on the stone and became like dead men. The angel's rolling the stone and sitting on it, resulting in the guards' becoming like dead men is one thing. The angel's talking to the women and inviting them to see the place where Jesus was laid was another thing. Matthew's record does not say that these events happened at the same time as if the guards were still there like dead men when the angel invited the women to see the place where Jesus was laid.

Alleged Contradiction # 86

86. Did anyone tell the women what happened to Jesus' body?
   (a) Yes. "A young man in a white robe" (Mark 16:5). "Two men … in dazzling apparel" later described as angels (Luke 24:4 and 24:23). An angel – the one who rolled back the stone (Matthew 16:2). In each case the women were told that Jesus had risen from the dead (Mathew 28:7; Mark 16:6; Luke 24:5 footnote)
   (b) No. Mary met no one and returned saying, "They have taken the Lord out of the tomb, and we do not know where they have laid him" (John 20:2)

Answer:

This question is based on the wrong assumption that all the ladies arrived at the tomb at the same time. This was not the case. John 20:1 says that Mary Magdalene arrived at the tomb "while it was still dark." The other ladies "came to the tomb when the sun had risen" (Mark 16:2). No angel told Mary that Jesus had risen from the dead. That's why her report to the disciples was that Jesus' body was taken away by some unknown persons.

Alleged Contradiction # 87

87. When did Mary Magdalene first meet the resurrected Jesus? And how did she react?
    (a) Mary and the other women met Jesus on their way back from their first and only visit to the tomb. They took hold of his feet and worshipped him (Matthew 28:9)
    (b) On her second visit to the tomb Mary met Jesus just outside the tomb. When she saw Jesus she did not recognize him. She mistook him for the gardener. She still thinks that Jesus' body is laid to rest somewhere and she demands to know where. But when Jesus mentioned her name she at once recognized him and called him "Teacher." Jesus said to her, "Do not hold me…" (John 20:11 to 17)

Answer:

The writer of *101 Contradictions in the Bible* is contradicting himself in this 87th Alleged Contradiction in the Bible. In letter (a) he says that Mary and the other women made "their first and only visit to the tomb." In (b) he says that Mary did a "second visit to the tomb."

As explained in the answer to question No. 86, Mary Magdalene and the other ladies did not arrive at the tomb at the same time. Mary arrived first and then reported to the disciples about the "lost" body of Jesus (John 20:1,2). So, when the other ladies left the tomb and met Jesus, Mary was not among them. Mary was back in the tomb (after Peter and John had gone to the tomb and examined what she reported) and met Jesus. Jesus then, after ascending to the Father, met the ladies who were still on their way to the apostles. Mary also went to the apostles, for the second time, to report of her encounter with Jesus (John 20:18). To list down the order of events at the tomb in relation to Mary Magdalene, the other ladies and Peter and John, here it is:

1. Mary Magdalene at the tomb while still dark, found the tomb empty and ran to report to the apostles. John 20:1,2

2. Acting upon Mary's report, Peter and John ran to examine the tomb and then left. John 20:3-10

3. The other ladies arrived when the sun was up and left the tomb with the angel's message. Mark 16:2-8, Matthew 28:5-8

4. Mary Magdalene back in the tomb and met Jesus. John 20: 11-17

5. The other ladies, still on their way to the apostles, met Jesus who presumably had already gone to the Father in heaven because He did not object to them holding His feet to worship Him. Matthew 28:9, 10

Alleged Contradiction # 88

88. What was Jesus' instruction for his disciples?
    (a) "Tell my brethren to go to Galilee, and there they will see me" (Matthew 28:10)
    (b) "Go to my brethren and say to them, I am ascended to my Father and your Father, to my God and your God" (John 20:17)

Answer:

Let's read the full verses of Scriptures referred to by this Alleged Contradiction:

(Mat 28:10) Then Jesus said to them, "Do not be afraid. Go *and* tell My brethren to go to Galilee, and there they will see Me." NKJV

(Joh 20:17) Jesus said to her, "Do not cling to Me, for I have not yet ascended to My Father; but go to My brethren and say to them, 'I am ascending to My Father and your Father, and *to* My God and your God.' "NKJV

The two verses above indeed have two completely different instructions. We can see why they're not the same.

Matt. 28:10 was addressed by Jesus to "them" - the women who were on their way to the disciples to report what the angel had told them at the tomb. So this encounter with Jesus would be an additional report to the what the angel had told them earlier. On the other hand, John 20:17 was addressed to "her" (Mary Magdalene) when she came back to the tomb after having reported Jesus' "missing body" to the disciples Peter and John (John 20:2-17).

In John 20:17, Jesus was still to go up to the Father immediately after His resurrection, (not the same as His ascension in the sight of His disciples which took place after having stayed with them for 40 more days of teaching and instructions, Acts 1: 1-3, 9-12; Luke 24:50-52). Note: The place of ascension of Christ immediately after conversation with Mary happened in Jerusalem near His tomb where Mary was. The ascension after 40 days with His disciples happened in Mt. Olives (Acts 1:9-12). The town of Bethany mentioned in Luke 24:50-52 is in the mount of Olives.

Following this careful analysis of the events above, we conclude that John 20:17 instruction to Mary Magdalene happened first before Jesus went to the Father after His resurrection. This was when Mary went back to the tomb, following Peter and John who had left the place already (John 20: 10, 11). After going up to the Father, Jesus showed Himself to the other women (Matt. 28:10) who were on their way to the disciples and gave His own instruction which would be an addition to what the angels told them (Matt. 28:5-8). Jesus' instruction to Mary was before He ascended to the Father and, therefore, included about His ascension. His instruction to the other women was after His going to the Father.

Alleged Contradiction # 89

89. When did the disciples return to Galilee?
    (a) Immediately, because when they saw Jesus in Galilee "some doubted" (Matthew 28:17) This period of uncertainty should not persist.
    (b) After at least 40 days. That evening the disciples were still in Jerusalem (Luke 24:33). Jesus appeared to them there and told them, stay in the city until you are clothed with power on high" (Luke 24:49). He was appearing to them "during forty days" (Acts 1:3), and "charged them not to depart from Jerusalem, but to wait for the promise..." (Acts 1:4)

Answer:

The first answer above (a) is not right. The disciples did not return to Galilee "immediately." The apostles and many of Jesus disciples were still in Jerusalem the first Sunday after the resurrection as well as the following Sunday. On the first Sunday Jesus met with His disciples in the evening with Thomas absent (John 20:19-24). The following Sunday Jesus again met with His disciples with Thomas present (John 20:25-29). The certainty of Christ's resurrection was established among His disciples in Jerusalem during this time. After this, when Jesus met with His disciples in a mountain in Galilee, they worshipped Him but some doubted (Matt. 28:16, 17). Who were those who doubted? This meeting is believed by most Bible commentators as the one referred to by the Apostle Paul where about 500 were present (1 Cor. 15:6). Jesus was a Galilean as well as those of His apostles. Many believed in Him in Galilee, far from the influence of the temple priests and Jewish leaders in Jerusalem. While the apostles and some of Jesus' disciples remained in Jerusalem for many days after His crucifixion, most of the Galilean disciples of Jesus, confused and discouraged by Jesus' death in Jerusalem just like His apostles, must have returned immediately to Galilee. They departed home without resolving their doubts and questions about the Messiah they thought would begin His reign as King of Israel. So when they met Jesus along with the apostles and the other disciples in a mountain in Galilee, some of them still doubted.

The second answer (b) is again not right. After 40 days, Jesus's disciples were not in Galilee but were again in the area of Jerusalem because of another Jewish festival, the Feast of Pentecost. "From the sixteenth of the month of Nisan (the second day of the Passover), seven complete weeks, i.e., forty-nine days, were to be reckoned, and this feast was held on the fiftieth day."[111] Forty days after Christ's resurrection, He was with His disciples in Bethany (Luke 24:50-53) in a mountain called Mt. Olives (or Olivet) (Acts 1:12) east of and facing Jerusalem. "The last appearance of Jesus occurred when he ascended to heaven from the Mount of Olives near Jerusalem."[112] Here Jesus Christ told them to wait for the promised Holy Spirit in Jerusalem after which He ascended to heaven (Acts 1:3-12; Luke 24:45-49). Ten days after that, on the day of Pentecost, the fiftieth day from Christ's resurrection, the Holy Spirit descended on the 120 disciples gathered in Jerusalem (Acts 1:15, 2:1-4).

---

[111]M.G. Easton (Author), *Easton's Bible Dictionary* Paperback, Printed by CreateSpace, An Amazon.com Company, (Publisher: CreateSpace Independent Publishing Platform, 2015) Entry on Pentecost

[112]Hendriksen and Kistemaker, *New Testament Commentary Set*, 12 Volumes, Notes on Acts 1:1-5

Alleged Contradiction # 90

90. To whom did the Midianites sell Joseph?
    (a) "To the Ishmaelites" (Genesis 37:28)
    (b) "To Potiphar, an officer of Pharoah" (Genesis 37:36)

Answer:

Let us read the full verse references being used in this Alleged Contradiction. Here they are:

(Gen 37:28) Then Midianite traders passed by; so *the brothers* pulled Joseph up and lifted him out of the pit, and sold him to the Ishmaelites for twenty *shekels* of silver. And they took Joseph to Egypt. NKJV

(Gen 37:36) Now the Midianites had sold him in Egypt to Potiphar, an officer of Pharaoh *and* captain of the guard. NKJV

Genesis 37:28 does not say that the Midianites sold Joseph to the Ishmaelites. What this verse says is that Joseph was pulled out of the pit by his brothers and sold to the Ishmaelites. The author of this Alleged Contradiction to the Bible must be trying to note that the words "the brothers" in this verse are written in italics and therefore do not appear in the original Hebrew. He, therefore, concluded that the Midianites were the ones who pulled Joseph up out of the pit and sold him to the Ishmaelites. This conclusion, though, would contradict the context of the narrative because the two verses immediately preceding this particular verse says: "(Gen 37:26) So Judah said to his brothers, "What profit *is there* if we kill our brother and conceal his blood? (Gen 37:27) Come and let us sell him to the Ishmaelites, and let not our hand be upon him, for he *is* our brother *and* our flesh. And his brothers listened." It is clear in these preceding two verses that it is not the Midianites but Joseph's brothers who wanted to sell him to the Ishmaelites.

In this verse (Genesis 37:28) both terms, Midianites and Ishmaelites, refer to the same group of people. Here's an explanation from *The Bible Knowledge Commentary*:

"Judah then prompted his brothers to sell Joseph to passing Ishmaelites on their way from Gilead... to Egypt. Ishmaelites were descendants of Abraham by Hagar (Gen 16:15) and the Midianites (Gen 37:28) descended from Abraham by his concubine Keturah (Gen 25:2). The term Ishmaelites became a general designation for desert tribes, so that Midianite traders were also known as Ishmaelites."[113]

Gill has this addition:

"Then there passed by Midianites, merchantmen,.... The same with the Ishmaelites before mentioned, as appears from the latter part of this verse; for as these were near neighbours, so they might join together in merchandise, and travel in company for greater safety, and are some-times called the one, and sometimes the other, as well as they might mix together in their habitations and marriages; and are hence called Arabians by the Targums, as before observed, and so by Josephus, which signifies a mixed people:"[114]

Here is a Bible verse showing that the names of these two groups of people are used to refer to the same people at times in the ISV and NET Bible versions:

(Jdg 8:24) But Gideon also added, "I would like to ask that each of you give me a ring from his war booty" because, as Ishmaelites, the Midianites had been wearing gold rings. ISV

(Jdg 8:24) Gideon continued, "I would like to make one request. Each of you give me an earring from the plunder you have taken." (The Midianites had gold earrings because they were Ishmaelites.) NET

---

[113]John R. Walvoord (Editor) and Roy B. Zuck, *The Bible Knowledge Commentary-An Exposition of the Scriptures by Dallas Seminary Faculty-New Testament*, Notes on Genesis 37:25-28

[114]Gill, *Exposition of the Entire Bible,* Notes on Genesis 37:28

With this understanding of Scriptures, we cannot say that the Medianites sold Joseph to the Ishmaelities as stated above in this alleged contradiction in the Bible.

Alleged Contradiction # 91

91. Who brought Joseph to Egypt?
    (a) The Ishmaelites bought Joseph and then "took Joseph to Egypt" (Genesis 37:28)
    (b) "The Midianites had sold him in Egypt" (Genesis 37:36)
    (c) Joseph said to his brothers "I am Joseph your brother whom you sold into Egypt" (Genesis 45:4)

Answer:

The answers for (a) and (b) under this question have been adequately answered in the answer or explanation under Alleged Contradiction No. 90. So let's comment on (c)of No. 91 question.

Yes, the brothers of Joseph sold him into Egypt according to Gen. 45:4. Since Joseph's brothers were not traders who went to sell their goods to Egypt, they accomplished this desire of selling Joseph to Egypt indirectly by selling him to the traders passing by who were going to Egypt. These traders were the Midianites who were also called Ishmaelites during that time.

Alleged Contradiction # 92

92. Does God change his mind?
    (a) Yes. "The word of the Lord came to Samuel: "I repent that I have made Saul King..." (I Samuel 15:10 to 11)
    (b) No. God "will not lie or repent; for he is not a man, that he should repent" (I Samuel 15:35). Notice that the above three quotes are all from the same chapter of the same book! In addition, the Bible shows that God repented on several other occasions:
        i. "The Lord was sorry that he made man" (Genesis 6:6). " I am sorry that I have made them" (Genesis 6:7)
        ii. "And the Lord repented of the evil which he thought to do to his people" (Exodus 32:14).
        iii. (Lots of other such references).

Answer:

Here's from Jamieson, Fausset and Brown:

"<u>1Sa 15:10</u>, <u>1Sa 15:11</u>. *God rejects him for disobedience.*

Then came the word of the Lord unto Samuel, saying, It repenteth me that I have set up Saul — Repentance is attributed in Scripture to Him when bad men give Him cause to alter His course and method of procedure, and to treat them as if He did "repent" of kindness shown."[115]

From Spence and Exell:

---

[115]Jamieson, Fausset and Brown, *Jamieson, Fausset, and Brown's Commentary on the Whole Bible,* Notes on 1 Samuel 15:10-11

"**It repenteth me**. By the law of man's free will his concurrence is necessary in carrying out the Divine purpose, and consequently every man called to the execution of any such purpose undergoes a probation. God's purpose will be finally carried out, but each special instrument, if it prove unworthy, will be laid aside. This change of administration is always described in Scriptural language as God's repentance, possibly because the phrase contains also the idea of the Divine grief over the rebellious sinner."[116]

God indeed does not change in His character. He deals with man according to His truth and righteousness. God's good plans and purposes for man is one thing. The fulfillment of those plans and purposes is another thing because God considers the free will of man, his obedience and cooperation to the will of God. That is why in Matt. 6:10, man is to pray that God's will be done or fulfilled in their lives on earth. When God planned the destruction of Nineveh because of their wickedness (Jonah 1:1,2), informed them about it through Jonah (Jonah 3:4) and then the people repented of their ways (chose to change their ways) (Jonah 3:5-9), the Lord also changed His plan for destruction (Jonah 3:10). God's character of love and justice has not changed in this case. What He actually does to men according to their response and obedience to Him is the one that changes. If God does not change in His dealings with men in relation to their responses to Him, then He becomes unjust and unrighteous and unforgiving. "God deals with us one way when we sin, and He changes His relationship when we repent and believe."[117]

---

[116]Spence and Exell, *The Pulpit Commentary,* Notes on I Sam. 15:11

[117]Elmer L. Towns, *Bible Answers for Almost All Your Questions*. (Nashville: Thomas Nelson Publishers, 2003). 278

Alleged Contradiction # 93

93. The Bible says that for each miracle Moses and Aaron demonstrated the magicians did the same by their secret arts. Then comes the following feat:
    (a) Moses and Aaron converted all the available water into blood (Exodus 7:20-21)
    (b) The magicians did the same (Exodus 7:22). This is impossible, since there would have been no water left to convert into blood.

Answer:

From Clarke's Bible commentary: "**And the magicians - did so -** But if all the water in Egypt was turned into blood by Moses, where did the magicians get the water which they changed into blood? This question is answered in Exo_7:24. The Egyptians dug round about the river for water to drink, and it seems that the water obtained by this means was not bloody like that in the river: on this water therefore the magicians might operate."[118]

Here's more explanations from Bible Knowledge Commentary: "Pharaoh's **magicians,** however, were able to duplicate this miracle, so he hardened his **heart** toward God. If all the water became blood, where did the magicians obtain water to duplicate the feat? The answer seems to be in Exo_7:24: the waters in the Nile were stricken but not the natural springs or waters filtered through the soil. The people had to abandon the Nile in order to have water to drink."[119]

---

[118]Clarke, *Adam Clarke's Commentary on the Bible*, Notes on Exodus 7:22

[119]John R. Walvoord (Editor) and Roy B. Zuck, *The Bible Knowledge Commentary-An Exposition of the Scriptures by Dallas Seminary Faculty-New Testament*, Notes on Exodus 7:22-25

94. Who killed Goliath?
     (a) David (I Samuel 17:23, 50)
     (b) Elhanan (2 Samuel 21:19)

Answer:

NET commentary has this explanation:

"The parallel passage in 1Ch_20:5 reads, "Elhanan son of Jair killed Lahmi the brother of Goliath." ...The Chronicles text has misread "Bethlehemite" (יְמִחְלַה תיבֵ, *bet hallakhmi*) as the accusative sign followed by a proper name אֶת לְחְמִי (*'et lakhmi*). (See the note at 1Ch_20:5.) The Samuel text misread the word for "brother" (חאָ, *'akh*) as the accusative sign (תאֶ, *'et*), thereby giving the impression that Elhanan, not David, killed Goliath. Thus in all probability the original text read, "Elhanan son of Jair the Bethlehemite killed the brother of Goliath."[120] So the one killed in this verse is not Goliath but his brother.

MacArthur further explains on 2 Samuel 21:19: "**Elhanan...killed the brother of Goliath.** The minor scribal omission of "the brother of" (in the Hebrew) belongs in this verse, based on 1Ch_20:5 which includes them, and because the Scripture says clearly that David killed Goliath as recorded in 1Sa_17:50.[121] For this reason Bible translations such as the NIV, NET, NLT and NKJV inserts "the brother of" before the word "Goliath."

---

[120]Biblical Studies Press (author), *NET Bible Full Notes Edition*, Notes on 2 Samuel 21:19

[121]MacArthur, *The MacArthur Bible Commentary*, Notes on 2 Samuel 21:19

God inspired the authors writing the original manuscripts but not the thousands of zealous copyists making copies of the original writings. He allowed these scribal errors so that godly truth seekers would be able to use their God-given abilities to research and to analyze. Prov. 25:2 applies here: "It is the glory of God to conceal a matter, But the glory of kings is to search out a matter" (NASB). The Message Bible applies this verse to our modern situation: "God delights in concealing things; scientists delight in discovering things" (MSG).

95. Who killed Saul?
    (a) "Saul took his own sword and fell upon it... Thus Saul died.. (I Samuel 31:4-6)
    (b) An Amalekite slew him (2 Samuel 1:1-16)

Answer:

This is the account of the death of King Saul according to 1 Samuel 31:3-6:

1Sa 31:3 The fighting grew fierce around Saul, and when the archers overtook him, they wounded him critically.

1Sa 31:4 Saul said to his armor-bearer, "Draw your sword and run me through, or these uncircumcised fellows will come and run me through and abuse me." But his armor-bearer was terrified and would not do it; so Saul took his own sword and fell on it.

1Sa 31:5 When the armor-bearer saw that Saul was dead, he too fell on his sword and died with him.

1Sa 31:6 So Saul and his three sons and his armor-bearer and all his men died together that same day.

In this account, we do not find about an Amalekite slaying King Saul. It is therefore clear that the Amalekite, knowing that David would be the next king of Israel, invented his story to get some favor when David becomes king of Israel, thinking that David would be happy to see his rival king dead. This was his fatal mistake because David respected King Saul even in his death and thus, the Amalekite was killed for claiming to have killed King Saul based on his fraudulent confession. At this point in time, David without the benefit of more sources of information about King Saul's death, may have taken the report of the Amalekite as true. Whether the Amalekite's testimony was true or not, David knew that the Amalekite, according to his report, had no respect for a man anointed by God, thus earning him the death penalty.

Jamieson, Fauset and Brown agree with the answer above with this commentary on 2 Samuel 1:2-12:

"The Amalekite, however, judging him to be actuated by a selfish principle, fabricated a story improbable and inconsistent, which he thought would procure him a reward."[122]

---

[122]Jamieson, Fausset and Brown, *Jamieson, Fausset, and Brown's Commentary on the Whole Bible,* Notes on 2 Samuel 1:2-12

Alleged Contradiction # 96

96. Does every man sin?
    (a) Yes, "There is no man who does not sin" (I Kings 8:46; see also 2 Chronicles 6:36; Proverbs 20:9; Ecclesiastes 7:20 and 1 John 1:810)[sic, might be 8-10]
    (b) No. True Christians cannot possibly sin, because they are the children of God. "Every one who believes that Jesus is the Christ is a child of God. (I John 5:1). "We should be called children of God; and so we are" (I John 3:1). "He who loves is born of God" (I John 4:7). "No one born of God commits sin; for God's nature abides in him, and he cannot sin because he is born of God" (I John 3:9). But, then again, Yes! "If we say we have no sin we deceive ourselves, and the truth is not in us" (I John 1:8)

Answer:

The person who asks this question has a wrong understanding here about the Christian doctrine of sin. The Bible does not teach that **a** child of God cannot sin anymore. Jesus Christ is THE Son of God. He was sinless when living as a man on earth. Only He is THE Son of God. Those who give their lives to Christ to follow Him are called children of God (John 1:12, 1 John 3:1 etc.), but they are ADOPTED children of God (Eph. 1:5, Gal. 4:5). As adopted sons and daughters of God, they grow from faith to faith (Rom. 1:17), from glory to glory (2 Cor. 3:18) to becoming more and more conformed to the image of Christ (Rom. 8:29). Though they grow spiritually day by day, they never attain sinless perfection on earth. This perfection for them is still to come (1 Cor. 13:10) and this will happen when Christ comes back and takes them to heaven with Him (1 Thess. 4:16,17). So, saying that true Christians cannot sin because they are children of God just like Jesus is the Son of God is not a Scriptural teaching.

Another wrong understanding of the Christian teaching is based on 1 John 3:9 where it is held that he who is born of God or a child of God does not sin or does not commit sin. This interpretation is due to a lack of knowledge of the Greek language (the *koine* Greek) which was used to write the New Testament. In the *koine*, the kind of action of the verbs is more important than the time of action which is the case in English language. The kind of action of the verb in 1 John 3:9 ("he cannot sin") tells us that it is continuous or repetitive just like a habit. This tells us that the committing of sin in this verse is not continuous or habitual. The acts of sinning here is due to a failure (not wanting to do it in the first place) and not because it is a habit or a practice of sinning. The Greek language is so different from the English language so that many times it needs an interpretation rather than just a simple translation to get what the original language is actually saying. That is why this verse is translated by the International Standard Version as thus: (1Jn 3:9) "No one who has been born from God practices sin, because God's seed abides in him. Indeed, he cannot go on sinning, because he has been born from God." The New Living Translation puts it this way: (1Jn 3:9) "Those who have been born into God's family do not make a practice of sinning, because God's life is in them. So they can't keep on sinning, because they are children of God."

There is a vast difference between to sin and to keep on sinning or to habitually practice sin. True children of God can commit sin as a failure but not as a habitual and willful practice of sin. When a born again Christian sins as a failure, he feels a godly sorrow, leading him to repentance (2 Cor. 7:10). The grace of God also stirs up in his heart the desire to make it right and come to God for forgiveness, including a desire for restitution if necessary. Whereas, when an unbeliever commits sin, he does not have the feeling of sorrow nor a repentant attitude that would lead him to God for help, because the Holy Spirit is not in his heart to convict him of his sin.

Alleged Contradiction # 97

97. Who will bear whose burden?
    (a) "Bear one another's burdens and so fulfill the law of Christ" (Galatians 6:2)
    (b) "Each man will have to bear his own load" (Galatians 6:5)

Answer:

The Greek word used in Gal. 6:2 and translated "burdens" is not the same as the word used in Gal. 6:5 which is translated "burden" in the King James Version. That's why the other Bible versions translate this different Greek word with another English word. BKC comments on Gal. 6:5 and comparing the word used here with the word used in Gal. 6:2. Here it is:

"The Christian does in fact test himself by carrying **his own load.** This does not contradict Gal_6:2 because the reference there is to heavy, crushing, loads (*barē*) — more than a man could carry without help. In this verse a different Greek word (*phortion*) is used to designate the pack usually carried by a marching soldier. It is the "burden" Jesus assigns to His followers (cf. Mat_11:30). There are certain Christian responsibilities or burdens each believer must bear which cannot be shared with others. Jesus assured His disciples that such burdens were light."[123]

In answer to this alleged contradiction, we say that one's burdens or needs can be helped or borne by others but there's just one's certain responsibility that he cannot make others be responsible of and he's going to give accountability for that himself before God.

---

[123]John R. Walvoord (Editor) and Roy B. Zuck, *The Bible Knowledge Commentary-An Exposition of the Scriptures by Dallas Seminary Faculty-New Testament,* Notes on Gal. 6:5

98. How many disciples did Jesus appear to after his resurrection?
    (a) Twelve (I Corinthians 15:5)
    (b) Eleven (Matthew 27: 3-5 and Acts 1:9-26, see also Matthew 28:16; Mark 16: 14 footnote; Luke 24:9; Luke 24: 33)

Answer:

Jesus chose twelve people among His disciples and named them apostles (Luke 6:13). This group was many times (25 times in the New Testament) called just by the name "the Twelve" and not "twelve apostles" or "twelve disciples." "The Twelve" became a sort of a title of the group and not actually referring to the number of persons in that group. Stating it in another way, there should be a difference in meaning between the words "twelve apostles" and "The twelve."

Jamieson, Fauset and Brown explain this issue this way: "**the twelve** — The round number for "the Eleven" (<u>Luk 24:33</u>, <u>Luk 24:36</u>). "The Twelve" was their ordinary appellation, even when their number was not full. However, very possibly Matthias was present (<u>Act 1:22</u>, <u>Act 1:23</u>)."[124] When Jesus appeared to the apostles with Thomas this time, Luke 24:33 describes the number as "the eleven and those *who were* with them gathered together." Just after 32 days or less later, Matthias took Judas' place because he qualified as one of the men "who have accompanied us all the time that the Lord Jesus went in and out among us, beginning from the baptism of John to that day when He was taken up from us" (Acts 1:21-22). The "eleven" in letter (b)   above based on the gospel writers underscores the fall of Judas Iscariot through his betrayal

---

[124]Jamieson, Fausset and Brown, *Jamieson, Fausset, and Brown's Commentary on the Whole Bible,* Notes on 1 Cor. 15:5

of Jesus. The "twelve" of Apostle Paul in 1 Cor. 15:5 written much later takes into consideration Matthias who was always with the apostles "all the time that the Lord went in and out" among them.

Alleged Contradiction # 99

99. Where was Jesus three days after his baptism?
   (a) After his baptism, 'the spirit immediately drove him out into the wilderness, And he was in the wilderness forty days... (Mark 1:12-13)
   (b) Next day after the baptism, Jesus selected two disciples. Second day: Jesus went to Galilee - two more disciples. Third day: Jesus was at a wedding feast in Cana in Galilee (see John 1:35; 1:43; 2:1-11)

Answer:

The writer of "*101 Contradictions in the Bible*" says in letter (a) above that after Jesus' baptism, "the spirit drove him out into the wilderness. And he was in the wilderness forty days... (Mark 1:12-13)." This is what Jesus actually did immediately after His baptism in water by John the Baptist.

The writer's claim in letter (b) is that the "Next day after baptism, Jesus selected two disciples." The writer also claims that on the second day after His baptism, Jesus went to Galilee and got two more disciples and that the following day (the third day, he claims) Jesus was in a wedding in Cana in Galilee. While in the three supporting verses cited by the writer we can read "the next day," (John 1:35) "the following day" (John 1:43) and "on the third day" (John 2:1), these events did not happen in their right sequence immediately after Jesus' baptism. In fact, John the apostle did not write anything about the baptism of Jesus in the Jordan and the forty-day temptation after that which Matthew, Mark and Luke already recorded much earlier before John's gospel. So, how can these three verses in John be following the event of the baptism of Jesus?

To see the proper sequence of events let us consider the following scriptures.

Mark 1:23-13 tells us where Jesus went to and what He did there after His baptism in water: He went into the wilderness and was tempted by the devil for 40 days. This is also mentioned in Matthew 4: 1-12 and Luke 4:1-13. The accounts of the event (Jesus' temptation in the wilderness) in Matthew and Luke are both immediately preceded by Jesus being baptized by John the Baptist (Matthew 3: 13-17 and Luke 3:21,22). Therefore, there is no doubt that after Jesus' baptism, He went into the wilderness and was tempted by the devil there.

To show that the claims of the writer of *"101 Contradictions in the Bible"* in (b)   is not according to the actual sequence in Scriptures, let us study carefully John 1:19-39 below.

Joh 1:19 Now this is the testimony of John, when the Jews sent priests and Levites from Jerusalem to ask him, "Who are you?"

Joh 1:20 He confessed, and did not deny, but confessed, "I am not the Christ."

Joh 1:21 And they asked him, "What then? Are you Elijah?" He said, "I am not." "Are you the Prophet?" And he answered, "No."

Joh 1:22 Then they said to him, "Who are you, that we may give an answer to those who sent us? What do you say about yourself?"

Joh 1:23 He said: "I *am* 'THE VOICE OF ONE CRYING IN THE WILDERNESS: "MAKE STRAIGHT THE WAY OF THE LORD," ' as the prophet Isaiah said."

Joh 1:24 Now those who were sent were from the Pharisees.

Joh 1:25 And they asked him, saying, "Why then do you baptize if you are not the Christ, nor Elijah, nor the Prophet?"

Joh 1:26 John answered them, saying, "I baptize with water, but there stands One among you whom you do not know.

Joh 1:27 It is He who, coming after me, is preferred before me, whose sandal strap I am not worthy to loose."

Joh 1:28 These things were done in Bethabara beyond the Jordan, where John was baptizing.

Joh 1:29 The next day John saw Jesus coming toward him, and said, "Behold! The Lamb of God who takes away the sin of the world!

Joh 1:30 This is He of whom I said, 'After me comes a Man who is preferred before me, for He was before me.'

Joh 1:31 I did not know Him; but that He should be revealed to Israel, therefore I came baptizing with water."

Joh 1:32 And John bore witness, saying, "I saw the Spirit descending from heaven like a dove, and He remained upon Him.

Joh 1:33 I did not know Him, but He who sent me to baptize with water said to me, 'Upon whom you see the Spirit descending, and remaining on Him, this is He who baptizes with the Holy Spirit.'

Joh 1:34 And I have seen and testified that this is the Son of God."

Joh 1:35 Again, the next day, John stood with two of his disciples.

Joh 1:36 And looking at Jesus as He walked, he said, "Behold the Lamb of God!"

Joh 1:37 The two disciples heard him speak, and they followed Jesus.

Joh 1:38 Then Jesus turned, and seeing them following, said to them, "What do you seek?" They said to Him, "Rabbi" (which is to say, when translated, Teacher), "where are You staying?"

Joh 1:39 He said to them, "Come and see." They came and saw where He was staying, and remained with Him that day (now it was about the tenth hour). NKJV

In the account above, John 1:29 says, "The next day John saw Jesus coming toward him, and said, "Behold! The Lamb of God who takes away the sin of the world!" The writer of *"101 Contradictions in the Bible"* claims this is the first day after Jesus was baptized in water. This is not so. If you read the verses immediately before this (verses 19-28) you will not find the account of Jesus' baptism in water. What we read here is the discussion between John the Baptist and the priests and Levites from Jerusalem (v. 19) and also with the Pharisees (v. 24). So, Jesus' coming toward John in John 1:29 does not come after His baptism but after the discussion of John the Baptist with the religious officials sent from Jerusalem.

In John 1:35-36, John again sees Jesus walking and declared the same words about Jesus. Verse 35 opens with "again, the next day, John..." This time, John's declaration about Jesus was in the hearing of two of his disciples. This happens on the second day, again, after his discussion with the Jews sent from Jerusalem and not second day after the baptism of Jesus.

The writer of *"101 Contradictions in the Bible"* also thinks that on the third day after His baptism, Jesus went to the wedding in Cana in Galilee. When did Jesus go to Galilee? John 1:43 says, "The following day Jesus wanted to go to Galilee, and He found Philip and said to him, "Follow Me." Now the question here is this: The "following day" of what? We find in the verses immediately before this (John 1:40-42), that Andrew, one of the two disciples of John who followed Jesus and slept that day in His quarter led his brother Simon Peter to Jesus. So, according to the preceding context, the "following day" here when Jesus went to Galilee, was the day after His encounter with Simon Peter. Following this encounter with Peter, Jesus went to Galilee (verse 43) where He got another disciple named Philip. Note that this encounter of Jesus with Philip could be Jesus' first day in Galilee. Philip then introduced Nathanael to Jesus (verses 44-51). This could be the second day in Galilee. Then in the verse immediately following this (next to verse 51), we read John 2:1,2 which says:

"Joh 2:1 On the third day there was a wedding in Cana of Galilee, and the mother of Jesus was there.

Joh 2:2 Now both Jesus and His disciples were invited to the wedding."

The third day, therefore, at the wedding of Cana in Galilee was the third day of Jesus in Galilee and not the third day after His baptism in water.

The lesson we get here when interpreting Scriptures is that we need to see what events happened before a verse of scripture and what events follow it in order to get the picture of how events probably unfolded. This is called interpretation according to the context.

Alleged Contradiction # 100

100. Was baby Jesus' life threatened in Jerusalem?
    (a) Yes, so Joseph fled with him to Egypt and stayed there until Herod died (Matthew 2:13-23)
    (b) No. The family fled nowhere. They calmly presented the child at the Jerusalem temple according to the Jewish customs and returned to Galilee (Luke 2:21-40)

Answer:

Let us read Gill's notes on Luke 2:39:

"**they returned into Galilee**: not that they came from thence to Jerusalem, but from Bethlehem, where Mary gave birth, and her time for purification was now just expired: nor did they go now directly to Galilee; or, if they did, they soon came back again to Bethlehem, since here the wise men found them two years after; when by a divine warning, they went into Egypt, where they remained till Herod's death, and after came into the land of Israel, into the parts of Galilee, and dwelt at Nazareth; for which reason it is here called their own city."[125]

The account in Luke about the baby Jesus being brought to and presented in the temple at Jerusalem does not contradict the narration in Matthew chapter 2. Let us read Matthew's account to get the facts:

Mat 2:8 And he sent them to Bethlehem and said, "Go and search carefully for the young Child, and when you have found *Him,* bring back word to me, that I may come and worship Him also."

---

[125]Gill Notes on Luke 2:39

Mat 2:9 When they heard the king, they departed; and behold, the star which they had seen in the East went before them, till it came and stood over where the young Child was.

Mat 2:10 When they saw the star, they rejoiced with exceedingly great joy.

Mat 2:11 And when they had come into the house, they saw the young Child with Mary His mother, and fell down and worshiped Him. And when they had opened their treasures, they presented gifts to Him: gold, frankincense, and myrrh.

Mat 2:13 Now when they had departed, behold, an angel of the Lord appeared to Joseph in a dream, saying, "Arise, take the young Child and His mother, flee to Egypt, and stay there until I bring you word; for Herod will seek the young Child to destroy Him."

Mat 2:14 When he arose, he took the young Child and His mother by night and departed for Egypt,

Mat 2:15 and was there until the death of Herod, that it might be fulfilled which was spoken by the Lord through the prophet, saying, "OUT OF EGYPT I CALLED MY SON."

Mat 2:16 Then Herod, when he saw that he was deceived by the wise men, was exceedingly angry; and he sent forth and put to death all the male children who were in Bethlehem and in all its districts, from two years old and under, according to the time which he had determined from the wise men. NKJV

We notice in the account above that when the wise men came, Jesus was in the house (Matt. 2:11) and not in a manger as recorded in Luke 2:16. When Herod saw that the wise men did not come back to report to him, he ordered the killing of the children from two years old and under (Matt. 2:16). This tells us that Jesus was about two years old when the wise men visited Him and when He and Mary were taken by Joseph to Egypt to escape the killings ordered by Herod. He was not an infant when Joseph brought Him to Egypt. Matthew's account then does not contradict that of Luke who narrated Jesus being brought to the temple in Jerusalem when He was yet a baby. According to Jewish laws in the

Old Testament for a new male child born, his mother is to present him before the Lord after her days of purification which is 40 days after the birth of the child.[126] After Jesus was presented in the temple in Jerusalem, His family went back to Galilee. Sometime within the span of two years, Joseph and Mary with Jesus went to Bethlehem again, their place of birth when the wise men visited them and, after that, was warned by an angel to flee to Egypt.

---

[126]Ibid Notes on Luke 2:22

Alleged Contradiction # 101

101. When Jesus walked on water how did the disciples respond?
    (a) They worshipped him, saying, "Truly you are the Son of God" (Matthew 14:33)
    (b) "They were utterly astounded, for they did not understand about the loaves, but their hearts were hardened" (Mark 6:51-52)

Answer:

Let's read the two passages cited above:

(Mat 14:33) Then those who were in the boat came and worshiped Him, saying, "Truly You are the Son of God."

Mar 6:51 Then He went up into the boat to them, and the wind ceased. And they were greatly amazed in themselves beyond measure, and marveled.

Mar 6:52 For they had not understood about the loaves, because their heart was hardened. NKJV

In the question above letter (b), the quote "utterly astounded" is taken from English Standard Version. In the NKJV the Greek words in the original language is translated "greatly amazed in themselves beyond measure, and marveled." Actually there are more than two Greek words here in the original language as written by Mark. NIV translation for these Greek words is: "completely amazed". NASB is: "utterly astonished." But let's read the literal Bible versions: AMP: "astonished exceedingly [beyond measure]," LITV (Literal Translation of the Holy Bible): "amazed, exceedingly beyond measure within themselves, and marveled," YLT (Young's Literal Translation): "greatly out of measure were they amazed in themselves, and were wondering," WUEST: "exceedingly beyond measure, in themselves they were amazed." Couldn't we see here that the disciples' being "greatly amazed... beyond measure... and marveled" in Mark in response to Jesus' walking on the water and of the wind stopping as He entered into the boat, would be expressed by them in worship and say as in Matthew's account, "Truly You are the Son of God!?" Then Mark immediately made a comment that in the previous miracle of Jesus' multiplying the bread and feeding five thousand men besides women and children which immediately preceded this miracle, the disciples' hearts were hardened and did not make this same kind of response to Jesus' miracle of walking on the water and calming the sea. So, the accounts in Matthew and Mark are not in contradiction but, together, make a fuller and better description of what actually happened.

Conclusion

The Bible as written by the original God-inspired writers is true and without contradictions.

The seeming contradictions in the Bible translations arise when any or a combination of these conditions exists:

1. Lack of understanding of the culture when the Bible was written. The Bible was written more than a thousand years ago, in an Oriental land that is diverse in its language, traditions and customs. Lack of understanding of the Biblical cultural background would lead to seeming contradictions in the Bible. An example is Alleged Contradiction # 52.

2. Interpretation of a Scripture verse not according to its context. A scripture passage is part of a whole narrative or a logical presentation, and without considering this factor, seeming contradictions would result. An example is Alleged Contradiction # 99.

3. Lack of understanding of the possible events surrounding an event. Giving consideration to other events mentioned in the same book and in other books of the Bible as well as previous events that are related to a newer event would solve seeming contradictions. An example is found in related alleged contradictions # 2 and # 3.

4. Lack of consideration of all available copies of the original manuscripts of the Bible and the different early translations of the Scriptures into contemporary languages like the Syriac, Arabic, or Greek (LXX translation

of the Old Testament) would lead to inaccurate translations in some Bible versions, especially the older ones. For an example, see Alleged Contradiction # 11.

5. Wrong understanding of the teaching on the inspiration of the Holy Scriptures. God inspired the original writers as they wrote the original manuscripts. Scribes copying from the original manuscripts or copying from copies of the original manuscripts were not inspired by God. They are susceptible, therefore, to human errors. Comparing the many copies available to us today would yield to the most likely original rendering of a certain text, as it is most unlikely that most of the writers will err on the same word in the original text. Where the variance between copies concern numbers, logic and common sense can help decide to determine what was written in the original writings. See as an example Alleged Contradiction # 12.

6. Lack of understanding of the rules of grammar of the original languages used in writing the Holy Bible. Each language has many uniqueness that cannot be found in other languages. Simple literal translation of Biblical Hebrew and Greek into another language many times would fail to yield the exact or complete meaning as intended by a Biblical author. In these cases, we need the Bible versions that explain and not just translate a passage or, more importantly if possible, a direct understanding of the rules of grammar and interpretation of the original languages. An example is Alleged Contradiction # 96.

7. Wrong understanding of the Christian doctrines. A person with a set of beliefs not based on the Bible would see seeming contradictions in certain scriptures when compared to passages in the other books of the Bible. This is because of the lack of understanding of Christian doctrines which take into consideration the whole Bible and not just one or two scriptures or books of the Bible. See as an example Alleged Contradiction # 54.

8. The unreasonable conclusion that different renderings by different biblical authors of the same event means they are contradictory. The truth is they are complementary. A good example of this is alleged contradiction # 65.

My discovery of the answers to the Alleged Contradictions in the Bible has given me a greater conviction of the truthfulness and reliability of the Bible as God's revelation to man to make him ready for the judgment throne of God. My sincere desire for everyone who reads this book is that he will make himself ready for God's judgment day by believing in Him and living for Him according to what He has revealed in the Holy Bible.

BIBLIOGRAPHY

Barnes, Albert, *Barnes Notes on the Old and New Testaments (Fourteen volumes) 19th Edition* Ada, Michigan: Baker Publishing Group, 1983

Biblical Studies Press (author) *NET Bible Full Notes Edition* Richardson, Texas: Biblical Studies Press, LLC, 2006

Clarke, Adam *Adam Clarke's Commentary on the Bible* Nashville, Tennessee: Thomas Nelson publisher, 1997

Easton, M.G. (Author) *Easton's Bible Dictionary* Paperback Printed by CreateSpace, An Amazon.com Company, Publisher: CreateSpace Independent Publishing Platform, 2015

Fausset, A. R *Fausset's Bible Dictionary* Grand Rapids, MI: Zondervan Publishers, 1949

Geissler, Norman L, and Howe, Thomas *The Big Book of Bible Difficulties* Grand Rapids, Michigan: Baker Books, 1992

Gill, John, *Exposition of the Entire Bible* Seattle, Washington: Amazon Digital Services LLC, August 2, 2012

Hayford, Jack W. (General Editor *Spirit Filled Life Bible (NKJV)* Nashville: Thomas Nelson Publishers, 1991

Hendriksen, William (Author) and Kistemaker, Simon J. (Author) *New Testament Commentary Set*, 12 Volumes Ada, Michigan: Baker Academic of Baker Publishing Group, 2002

Jamieson, Robert, Brown, David, and Fausset, A.R. *A Commentary on the Old and New Testaments* Peabody: Hendrickson Publishers, 1997

Jamieson, Robert, Fausset, A.R. and Brown, David *Jamieson, Fausset, and Brown's Commentary on the Whole Bible* Grand Rapids, MI: Zondervan Publishers, 1999

Keener, Craiz S. (Author) *The IVP Bible Background Commentary: New Testament 02nd Edition* Downers Grove, IL: IVP Academic, 2014

Keil, Johann and Delitzsch, Franz *Keil & Delitzsch Commentary of the Old Testament* Peabody, MA: Hendrickson Publishers, 1996

MacArthur, John (author) *The MacArthur Bible Commentary* Nashville, Tennessee: Thomas Nelson publisher, 2005

MacDonald, William and Farstad, Arthur L. *Believer's Bible Commentary* Nashville, Tennessee: Thomas Nelson Publisher, 1995

MacLaren, Alexander (Author) *Expositions of Holy Scriptures* (Classic Reprint) London, UK: Forgotten Books, 2016

McGee, J Vernon (Author) *Thru the Bible, 5 Volumes* Nashville, Tennessee: Thomas Nelson Publisher, 1990

Nave, Orville J. *Nave's Topical Bible* Nashville, Tennessee: Southwestern Company, 1962

Oxford Reference, "Alexandrian World Chronicle." Available from http://www.oxfordreference.com/view/10.1093/oi/authority.20110803095401732. Internet; (accessed 20 December 2016)

Robertson, A.T. (Author), *Word Pictures in the New Testament (6 Vols.)* Ada, Michigan: Baker Publishing Group, 1982

Ryle, Herbert Edward *The Cambridge Bible for Schools and Colleges* Charleston, SC: BiblioBazaar, 2009

Schaff, Philip (Editor) *A Popular Commentary of the New Testament* New York: Charles Scribner's Sons, 1960

Spence, H D M. and Exell, J., *The Pulpit Commentary* Grand Rapids: Eerdmans Publishing Company, 1950

Strong, James (Author) *Strong Exhaustive Concordance of the Bible with Greek and Hebrew Dictionary* Nashville, TN: Crusade Bible Inc., 1990

Strong, James (author) *Strong's Exhaustive Concordance of the Bible with Greek and Hebrew Dictionaries* Peoria, IL: Royal Publishers, 1979

Torrey, RA *Treasury of Scripture Knowledge* Peabody: Hendrickson Publishers, 2002

Vincent, Marvin R. (Author) *Word Studies in the New Testament (4 Volume Set)* Grand Rapids, MI: Wm. B. Eerdmans Publishing Co, 1975

Vine, W.E. (Author), *Vine's Complete Expository Dictionary of Old and New Testament Words*

Nashville, Tennessee: Thomas Nelson publisher, 1996

Walton, John H., Matthews, Victor H. and Chavalas, Mark W. *The IVP Bible Background Commentary: Old Testament* Downers Grove, IL: IVP Academic, 2000

Walvoord, John R. (Editor) and Zuck, Roy B. *The Bible Knowledge Commentary-An Exposition of the Scriptures by Dallas Seminary Faculty-New Testament,* (Colorado Springs, CO: Chariot Victor Publishing, 1998

Walvoord, John F. (Editor) and Zuck, Roy B. (Editor) *The Bible Knowledge Commentary (Old Testament)* Wheaton, IL: Victor Books, 1985

Wellman, Jack *"What Language Did Jesus Speak? Was it Aramaic or Hebrew?"* http://www.patheos.com/blogs/christiancrier/2014/10/04/what-language-did-jesus-speak-was-it-aramaic-or-hebrew/ (accessed March 14, 2017)

Wiersbe, Warren W. (Author) *Wiersbe Bible Commentary NT Wiersbe Bible Commentaries* Colorado, Springs: David C. Cook, 2007

Article on *101 Contradictions in the Bible* online:

Media.isnet.org. http://media.isnet.org/kmi/off/XXtian/101ContradictionsInTheBible.pdf (Accessed April, 11, 2018)

Ebooks.rahnuma.org. http://ebooks.rahnuma.org/religion/
     Christianity/101%20Contradictions%20In%20The%20Bible.pdf
     (Accessed April 11, 2018)

Internationalindigenoussociety.com. http://
     internationalindigenoussociety.com/wp-content/
     plugins/pdfjs-viewer-shortcode/pdfjs/web/viewer.
     php?file=http%3A%2F%2Finternationalindigenoussociety.com%2Fwp-
     content%2Fuploads%2F2017%2F04%2F101-Contradictions-In-The-
     Bible.pdf&download=true&print=true&openfile=false (Accessed April
     11, 2018)

Sunnahonline.com. http://sunnahonline.com/ilm/dawah/0009.htm
     (Accessed April 11, 2018)

Answering-Christianity.com. http://www.answering-christianity.
     com/101_bible_contradictions.htm. (Accessed April 11, 2018)